So many powerful statements in *The Rebalancing Act*! From advocating to yourself and surrounding yourself with supportive family, friends, and colleagues, this book is a must-read for all working women, whether you're in your first year of employment or retirement is around the corner. What an outstanding book to share with my teams and to open the dialogue of personal journeys, conflicting priorities, and how we can organizationally support each other better.

COLLEEN MURPHY-SMITH

Vice President of Fuel Sales & Marketing, Motiva Enterprises LLC

Too many books about juggling the multiplicity of demands we face in life offer too many theories and not enough creative and practical "how-to" skills. Not this book! You'll discover great case studies of how you can, every day, be more effective in handling the challenges you face in life.

JOHN A. DALY

Liddell Professor of Communication & TCB Professor of Management, University of Texas at Austin, and award-winning author. (Also, winner of every campus-wide undergraduate teaching award at UT, and Carol and her daughter's favorite professor ever!)

Carol's book captivated me with its insightful exploration of various working women archetypes, resonating deeply with different phases of my career. This reflective narrative offers a profound introspection, guiding women to illuminate their past experiences, understand their present circumstances, and envision the futures they aspire to create. Through practical strategies, Carol empowers us to advocate for ourselves in today's dynamic workplaces, ensuring we lead purposeful and meaningful lives and careers.

POOJA PATANKAR

Leadership Coach and Talent Leader

Reading *The Rebalancing Act* brought me face-to-face with the pervasive and conflicting expectations women face in their quest to "have it all" and reminded me of my grandmother's remarkable journey. Much like the women Enneking describes, my grandmother balanced a demanding career with her family responsibilities. Throughout several career changes, she remained steadfast in her commitment to her professional aspirations while also striving to be a wonderful wife and raise her grandson—me. Enneking's archetypes resonate deeply with my grandmother's experiences. She was our family's Overloaded Olivia, constantly juggling the demands of work and home. Enneking's insights emphasize the importance of making mindful choices and setting realistic expectations. True fulfillment, as I've seen through my grandmother's experiences, comes from understanding our limits and making conscious decisions about what truly matters.

DAVON WILLIAMS

Producer, Actor, Writer

The Rebalancing Act shines light on something so many women fall prey to—holding ourselves to a higher standard, seeking approval, and expecting more from ourselves than we would ever expect from anyone else. As a wife, mother, and working professional, I felt the need to handle absolutely everything, trying to be present at work to climb the corporate ladder, be present for my children, and at the end of the day be present and spending quality time with my husband. Not only is this pace unrealistic, but it's also completely exhausting. I truly thought if I did it all, I could have it all! This book helped me realize that the one person I wasn't present for was me! It showed me by being present for me, the only approval I need is my own, and with boundaries I can still have it all without trying to do it all.

RENEE BACON

Senior Vice President, Sales & Operations & Chief Merchandising Officer, Murphy Oil

The Rebalancing Act is a powerful and timely exploration of women's roles in today's dynamic workforce. With courage and authenticity, it delves into managing conflicting priorities and carving out intentional, lasting legacies. A must-read for anyone seeking inspiration and practical wisdom to transcend societal expectations and achieve true balance in life and career.

BOB DILL

Retired CEO, Hisco; Managing Director, Lumen Institute

Reading *The Rebalancing Act* feels like you are surrounded by like-minded women who have learned to navigate and balance their competing priorities of work and personal life. Carol Enneking is a gifted and authentic writer who shares her wisdom from knowing firsthand what it takes to get to the top in a corporate world. Her brilliant insights will leave you feeling like it is time to reset and consider all the possibilities for success in your life as you realize your true potential. After reading the first chapter I began to write a list of women I want to share this inspiring book with, as I truly believe it will be transformational for women of all ages.

DENISE MCINTYRE

Founder and President of The Learning Edge

The balancing act between career, family, and personal aspirations is a continual tightrope walk. Carol's insights are not just timely but necessary, offering practical strategies to navigate our multifaceted lives. This book is a timely resource for women looking to redefine success on their terms!

MELISSA ORTIZ

Founder and CEO of Activate Human Capital Group

Carol Enneking's *The Rebalancing Act* is a game-changer for women in the workplace. With refreshing honesty and practical wisdom, Enneking dismantles the exhausting myth that women must "be it all to 'have it all." This book offers a transparent look at common pitfalls and a hopeful roadmap to authenticity, tested by dozens of successful women. Enneking's insights provide readers with actionable strategies to integrate their unique gifts into their work lives, creating a more fulfilling and balanced career. For any woman seeking to show up as her best self at work, *The Rebalancing Act* is an essential and empowering read.

THERESE WEBER

Vice President, Implementation Coaching at Challenger, Gray & Christmas, Inc.

In *The Rebalancing Act*, Carol uses her experience, plus those of dozens of other women, to present an honest and unvarnished picture of the challenges women experience when balancing different components of their lives. More importantly, she provides readers with specific and actionable strategies that have real meaning and effectiveness when trying to find that "right balance." I cannot emphasize enough the value that this book will bring to any woman trying to find the healthy balance of navigating both professional and family demands.

ROBERT WINTER

President, Trinity Training and Development

Carol Enneking is masterful in empowering women with the tools needed to succeed in taking their lives back. She provides humor as well as insight into her own struggles, which will help so many women feel that they are not alone.

SARAH SWINDELL

Autism Advocate and Author of *Rounding Home*

Carol provides invaluable insights on how to approach work and life when it's pulling you in multiple directions. She offers engaging relatable examples of problems, with compelling and thoughtful solutions. This book is a must-read for women as well as men who work with women.

JEFFREY L. FOSTER

CEO, Cimarron

The Rebalancing Act is an essential read for any woman looking for a helping hand in life. Enneking's insightful guide, with input from many, provides practical advice, empowering strategies, and real-life examples that address the unique challenges women face today. Whether you're advancing in your career or managing a busy household, whether young or mature, this book inspires harmony and success. It's an indispensable resource for every woman who needs a reminder that we are all on this journey together!

JANINE RANSKI

EVP Sales Head, United States, Intellect Design Arena Ltd

Carol's voice is genuine and thoughtful; her passion for authentic truth is immeasurable. Her playbook was crafted by tears of joy and sorrow and is meant for those who not only dare to dream, but for those who have the courage and strength to be vulnerable.

MATTY MALONE

President and Co-Founder, Simple Spirits Co.

Carol Enneking's *The Rebalancing Act* is a must-read for any working woman struggling to maintain a healthy work-life balance. Enneking's candid and insightful look at the challenges faced by women in the workplace, along with practical advice for navigating them, is both refreshing and empowering. As a fellow "Overloaded Olivia," I found this book incredibly relatable. It offers practical advice and strategies for setting boundaries, prioritizing tasks, and achieving a healthier work-life balance, which is something I desperately need!

DEBBIE RICHARDS

International Speaker and Chief Technology Officer at Creative Interactive Ideas

The Rebalancing Act is exquisite. This beautiful memoir wrapped in leadership is raw and honest while also connecting us as women. The way Carol shares her heart, experience, life, and truth will inspire you to live the life you are meant to, letting go of what no longer matters. This book will lift you up and awaken you to your freedom.

TRICIA BROUK

International award-winning director, author,
producer and Founder of The Big Talk Academy.

Enneking provides practical insights and powerful advice to women wondering how, and if, to "have it all." Her seven archetypes—from Perfect Paige to Overloaded Olivia—empathize with these common challenges and help her readers to strike their best balance.

MARC EFFRON

Best-selling author and President, Talent Strategy Group

Cheers to REBALANCING!
All the best,
Carol

THE
REBALANCING
ACT

WISDOM FROM WORKING WOMEN
FOR SUCCESS THAT MATTERS

CAROL ENNEKING
WITH BETHANY BRADSHER

THE BIG TALK PRESS

Library of Congress Control Number:

ISBN: Paperback 978-1-960553-01-0 eBook 978-1-960553-03-4 Hardcover 978-1-960553-04-1

Cover and interior design by Stephanie Whitlock Dicken.

THE BIG TALK *press*

DEDICATION

I dedicate this book, with love,
to those who have made me who I am:

MY MOTHER, MARGARET:

You raised me to aim high, provided a foundation of faith that has sustained me, and modeled grace, love, courage, hard work, dedication to family, integrity, and commitment. You are a tremendous role model and made me the person I am today.

MY CHILDREN, BRADLEY AND BETHANY:

You taught me what unconditional love truly felt like the day each of you entered this world, have blessed me beyond measure with the honor of raising you, and make my heart want to burst with pride that the Lord chose me to be your mom.

MY HUSBAND, ERIC:

You restored my faith in love and marriage, gave me a zest for life I never thought possible, have made me laugh more since I have met you than in all the days before, and love me so well that I never want to face a day without you.

Thank you for believing in me
and encouraging me on this journey.

TABLE OF CONTENTS

FOREWORD

Women are uniquely positioned to exert influence and find fulfillment in today's workplace, though this can be hard to see when we're consumed by the daily fray. Carol Enneking has a great ability to step back from the immediate challenges and help women identify the opportunities, as well as the challenges, that face them.

For decades, Carol has worked for large corporations, run her own companies, or provided services to organizations on a contract basis—all while raising a family, dealing with serious health issues, and going through divorce. So she knows firsthand the relentless tug-of-war women endure when they try to juggle too many things at once while also striving for perfection. Carol's ability to draw practical insights from her own rich and varied experience has given her clear and original insights into women's often complicated workplace journeys.

The Rebalancing Act offers a platform for Carol's hard-earned wisdom, as well as observations drawn from interviews with more than seventy working women of all ages and professional backgrounds. Carol understands that one size never fits all when it comes to helping working women reach their full potential, so her interviews expand the range of stories about traps that can limit women and offer a range of strategies we can use to overcome them.

Whether you're a woman in your first professional role or a seasoned leader with decades of experience, I am confident that you'll find yourself in these pages. My own work has focused on helping women recognize, articulate, and act on their greatest strengths and on helping organizations create more inclusive cultures in which women and others who have historically been underrecognized can reach their full potential. So, I am grateful to have a resource like *The Rebalancing Act*. We all need books that name our individual struggles as we seek balance and contentment. And we all need practical "how-tos" based on what has worked for others. Thanks to writers like Carol, we never have to walk this road alone.

Sally Helgesen, Best-selling Author, Speaker and Leadership Coach

"If you
choose
not to decide,
you still
have made
a choice."

"FREEWILL," RUSH

CHAPTER ONE

The Mythical Quest to "Have It All"

As women, one of the phrases we all hear time and time again is that we can and should want to "have it all." I have spent the last three decades chasing after this elusive dream of Having It All, and for much of that time I didn't fully understand what "It" even was. But after all this time, I am here to tell you I have finally discovered the answer. Before I share it with you, let's take a moment to review some of the prevalent messages I saw on TV regularly during my youth, my formative years. I am a child of the seventies and eighties, so my life growing up revolved around music and TV. I love music and can still belt out a tune from that time with the best of them! Just ask my kids and they will tell you. You will see many music and TV references in these pages.

Let's start with TV commercials in the seventies, like, "I can bring home the bacon, fry it up in a pan, and never ever let you forget you're a man." Okay, so I need to have an amazing, well-paying job, get the groceries, cook, and at the end of all that, be sexy for my man. What about the kids? Where do they fit into that equation? Hmmm. Then there's the deodorant commercial that said I should never let them see me sweat. So, keep my cool in all circumstances. Got it. If all that was too much, I could just hop in the tub and say, "Calgon, take me away!" to enjoy a relaxing bubble bath. I assume, in this scenario, my husband would magically care for the kids so I could relax. Because, according to the cigarette commercials, we've "come a long way baby!" Or have we? I'm starting to get confused here.

And now for my spoiler alert: the key to unlocking It All and making it ours. We cannot have it all, at least not at the same time. And we are exhausting ourselves trying. I am here to share what I have learned from my own quest for this elusive dream, and also to provide some insights into what I have learned from interviewing other working women of all ages about how they managed this seemingly impossible juggling act.

Figuring out the recipe for fulfillment involves working through countless contradictions. While the media for these messages have evolved since those commercials I saw in the seventies, young women today are still bombarded with conflicting messages in social media. Work like a boss, but party like a rock star. Embrace body positivity, but use this app to filter any imperfections before you post on social media. Live simply, but whip up this twenty-nine-ingredient recipe because it's the best ever. Don't work too hard, so you can strive for work-life balance. But be sure to make time for exotic vacations, Pinterest-worthy homes, and professional photos in your matching outfits. And people wonder why we are struggling to keep up with it all.

Women have more choices than ever before about how we spend our time, but just because we have choices does not mean we can avoid making any choices. We are fortunate to have these choices, thanks to the trailblazers who paved the way for us. But we must allow ourselves the opportunity to make choices and say no to some things, especially things that are of lower value. Women, in particular, seem to struggle with this notion of trying to do and have it all. We don't typically hear men talking about having it all. Avoiding making smart choices has led to an epidemic of stressed-out, burned-out, worn-out working women.

I have spent over thirty years living a life that was so filled with things to do that I had nothing left within me to be *fulfilled.* It took facing blindness and cancer for me to figure out how to rebalance my life. I fell into many of the traps that can consume us when we are not mindful of our choices.

When we examine this delicate balancing act, it is not surprising to learn that twenty-five percent of working women left the workforce during the pandemic. When any one of the balls we are juggling falls, like a childcare facility closing or a loved one needing extra care, the amount of effort it can take to rebalance can feel overwhelming. How can we make critical game-time decisions to keep life on track, not just for ourselves, but for those who depend on us?

I set out on a quest to talk with working women of all ages about the hard choices they made, about the things they have left behind so they could live right. Through this book, I will share their ideas with you. Here are a few examples of the conundrums my fellow working women have faced:

When Julia was a young lawyer, she was thriving in her position at a prestigious law firm in New York when she learned she was expecting her first child. Everyone in her office worked long hours every day, sometimes more than forty straight hours without a break. No one talked much about their personal lives, but Julia had a hunch that her news might not be embraced within the law firm's walls. More than a little apprehensive, Julia resolved to hide her pregnancy for as long as possible, until she finally had to tell her law firm's partners. Once she did, she was shocked when they told her that in the 100-plus years of the law firm's existence, there had never been a pregnant associate there.

The firm's partners seemed unsure about how to proceed, but no one mentioned cutting back on her workload. The grind of that firm became so exhausting for her during her pregnancy that she talked to her obstetrician about her concerns, and he wrote a note for her partners stating that she could not work more than fifteen hours without a break. The firm did not accept those terms, so Julia had to go on disability for the remainder of her pregnancy. After her son was born she attempted a work-from-home arrangement that was doomed to fail, because the firm remained completely inflexible. Soon she was looking for another job, but during her interviews with new firms, she said, "I really tried to hide the fact that I had children."

Fast forward several jobs and two more babies, and Julia, a single mother, decided to leave another high-powered position because she needed more margin in her life for her children. The job she was moving to wasn't as challenging or fulfilling as her previous position, but after trying to perfect the juggling act for years she had reached the conclusion that the career she wanted and the family she loved could not co-exist. At her going-away party, one of the managers who knew about Julia's family said, "Now she will be able to spend more time with her kids," and Julia heard multiple comments around the room from people who had no idea that she was a mother. That early experience at the law firm had so firmly convinced her that family life and professional accomplishments were incompatible for women that she had, for a time, constructed sturdy walls between the sectors of her life.

Camille has built a successful executive career, working up to several management positions despite considerable obstacles along the way. Every prospective job promotion was a battle, because the mostly male executives always assumed that she was a mother and therefore she would not have the time to devote to her job. Raise negotiations were likewise fraught, with Camille feeling like she had to defend her right to make the same salary as her male counterparts. She had to advocate for herself repeatedly, standing for other women who, like her, just want an opportunity to work hard and seek advancement.

Even though she has faced opposition throughout her career because of a perceived conflict with motherhood, Camille also made the significant decision to remain childless, because she felt that the demands of her workplace would not allow her to devote enough time to children. Her job required her to work night and weekend shifts and to be available for emergencies, and she could not reconcile those scheduling requirements with parenthood. She still has moments when she revisits that very difficult decision, and when she reflects on her path, she wishes that women could somehow pursue excellence in multiple arenas without having to compromise, or block access to, any of them.

At one point when she worked for a large company, Donna had a perpetually difficult time relating to her direct supervisor. She often heard from other employees that her manager had been saying negative things about her behind her back, but he almost never asked her for feedback or made any attempts to get to know her. When she inquired about the standards she would need to meet for promotion, he actually set different expectations and performance metrics for her than anyone else at her level was required to meet. Then, when she hit those metrics, he accused her of being entitled and arrogant, made her wait six months for a potential promotion, and then ultimately rejected recommending her for the new opportunity.

Mystified by this discouraging style of leadership, especially when neither Donna nor her coworkers could see any reason for her poor treatment, she asked for documentation for his claims that she was arrogant, closed to feedback, or an unwilling team player. No evidence was ever given, but Donna finally received something like a breakthrough when, in a short one-on-one conversation with her supervisor, he revealed that she reminded him of both his mother and his ex-wife. He had often badmouthed both women to employees in the company, and it seemed that in drawing a comparison between them and Donna, he had also adopted foregone, and false, conclusions about her capability within the company.

In an email to the company's leadership team, Donna aired her grievances about her unjust treatment, calling the management out on their failure to live into their stated organizational values of integrity, self-advocacy, and the elimination of biased and harassing behavior. Rather than receiving her admonishment and offering an apology, the leaders became defensive, and Donna submitted her resignation that very day.

AT LEAST SEVEN WAYS TO GET STUCK

Each of these is a true story, with only the names of the women changed, and each represents a specific type of dead end that can stop women who seek success in the workplace. I am pleased to share that these three women did successfully overcome difficult circumstances to find personal and professional fulfillment, but their journeys were more complicated than they needed to be. Whether it's through the impossibility of playing dozens of roles at home and at work, the challenge of longstanding biases in upper management, or a perpetual lack of understanding of what capable women can offer, honest glimpses like these prove that corporate America has made only halting progress in creating true opportunities for women, and the growth that has occurred too often looks like three steps forward and (at least) two steps back.

My own experience has given me a front-row seat to the pitfalls, and the opportunities to rise above those pitfalls, facing women pursuing career fulfillment. To help sketch out a blueprint of where we are and where we hope to go, I have created seven different archetypes of women in the workplace—caricatures of women who are not where they hope to be because of the myriad traps that litter the landscape of corporate America. For each of these seven types, aided by the honest assessment of more than seventy women and men interviewed for this book, I hope to illuminate the characteristics of each, the unique obstacles each has faced at work, and practical techniques to navigate around those roadblocks to the open road ahead.

If you are on this journey with me, you will undoubtedly see yourself, or your coworkers, family members, and friends, in these seven archetypes. This is not a personality assessment in the sense that every woman only falls into one category; it is likely that you have embodied more than one along your employment journey, and your association with these types might very well shift according to your age, specific job challenges, and stage of life. These fictional women are meant to aid you in understanding your own path with clarity and encourage you as you seek to overcome the mindsets, misunderstandings, and missteps that have led you to become stuck. Our seven archetypes, in brief, are:

☐ **Overloaded Olivia:** Olivia wears a dozen or more hats and scrambles through every day wondering how she can excel at any of them. Her work-life balance is non-existent, she can't sort her priorities when the urgent seems to constantly drown out the important, and she wonders how she ever succumbed to the myth of "having it all."

☐ **Perfect Paige:** Steeped in her desire to do all things well, Perfect Paige is capable, efficient, and intelligent, but she works better independently than on a team because she so fears making a mistake. She misses out on true connections with coworkers and clients and shows up wearing a facade that is impossible to maintain.

☐ **Cool Camryn:** Coworkers might label her as an "ice princess," but Cool Camryn is trying to find her way in her workplace by rising above both conflict and true community and just getting through the day. She is often an introvert by nature, but she comes off as guarded and stymied by the belief that vulnerability and emotion, if she let them show, would be liabilities to her professional life.

☐ **Trailblazer Tess:** Tess views the workplace as an arena for power plays, and she comes armed with tools that might help her prevail in the moment but will likely lead to unhealthy patterns in the long run. Whether it's the way she dresses, her temptation to act like a man to compete in a man's world, or a tough exterior she has put up due to mistreatment in the past, Tess struggles to show up with authenticity in a world that she fears cannot accept her genuine self.

- [ ] **Invisible Isabella:** Like Tess, Invisible Isabella may have had her voice silenced in the past, so she has learned to effectively silence herself. She keeps her head down, tells people what they want to hear, and sidesteps any true investment into the organization's mission. Detractors think that Isabella doesn't want to work hard, but her reluctance to engage in the workplace is more often a reaction to poor leadership and a lack of vision for her role within the organization.

- [ ] **Lovable Lila:** Everyone wants Lila on their team; she is adaptable, collaborative, and well-liked in every room. But her propensity to go along to get along and lack of leadership courage may impair her ability to influence coworkers and manage the interests of herself and others effectively.

- [ ] **Striving Sabrina:** Sabrina has her eye on the prize, but her drive to succeed can hinder her emotional, physical, and relational health in the workplace. She operates from a scarcity mentality and wants her share of success, but that misguided belief separates her from her coworkers and allows the spirit of competition to supplant teamwork and cooperation.

WHY YOU SHOW UP THE WAY YOU DO

Through an exploration of these seven workplace personas, I hope to give you plenty of connection points for understanding the travails and triumphs of your professional life so far. These seven composites can help women in every stage of their work journey excavate the past experiences, insecurities, and false beliefs that have caused them to act and react in unhealthy ways. Seeing your own behavior reflected in the description of **Tess, Sabrina, Camryn,** or the others is the first step, but determining your motivation for those behaviors and embracing new mindsets and habits to show up better is the ultimate goal.

My goal for this book is not to make a precise diagnosis for each reader, but instead to remind you that you're not alone as you navigate the wide range of challenges that will come up as you seek to excel professionally. I know what it's like to feel like I am the only person facing my particular circumstances, and I have found such tremendous value in solidarity and community as we travel these often-unpredictable roads. The women who have gone ahead of you carry wisdom that they are willing to share, and their stories are a reminder that you aren't alone and that as we integrate the experiences of others into our own, we can, with renewed strength, be part of changing the landscape for the better.

The women and men who agreed to give their time and transparency to my survey will be our true guides on this journey, and I will supplement their insights with stories and thoughts from my own story of thriving and stumbling in big corporations, small companies, and independent ventures. I have made so many of these mistakes myself, and I have come to realize that the past thirty-three years have been a vision quest of sorts—diverting my focus away from the type of person and employee I thought I "should" be to figuring out who I am and what I actually want.

At so many of the mileposts along my own journey, the details of which I will share with you in the personal chapters woven throughout this book, I have come to realize how untenable this balancing act truly is. Like most of you, I embraced the idea of having it all, and I strived to make that myth a reality, to no avail. As an employee in a huge corporation, a consultant, a business owner, a mother, a wife, a divorcee, a wife again, and a cancer survivor, I am grateful for every ounce of insight I have gained through the moments of gratification and the treacherous pitfalls I have faced.

Because of the courageous, wise women who have shared their stories and my own personal stories, I believe this book can offer you not only a transparent look at the ways we miss the chance to be our best selves in the workplace, but also a hopeful picture of how we can show up better.

If you approach this reading journey with honesty, you will be rewarded with a fresh perspective, a road map to authenticity tested by dozens of women before you, and a vision for the way your unique gifts and dreams can be fully integrated into your work life.

—w—

My Road

For a long time, others' expectations of me were so deeply ingrained in my self-image that I took those expectations as gospel instead of defining my own parameters for success, fulfillment, and happiness. I grew up in a family with parents who did a lot of things right, and for that I am thankful each day. I am not here to judge what they might have done better. They were not perfect, but being a parent myself, I know that none of us are!

I think we were the typical family of my generation. My parents started with nothing, ate a lot of pork and beans to make it in the early days, worked hard to provide for us, and gave us a good upbringing. We didn't have any huge family scandals or negative experiences, and I was fortunate to have two parents who wanted the best for us and cared very much about instilling values and teaching us right from wrong. My dad was somewhat typical of the times—an authority figure—and I feared him. I was scared to get in trouble, scared to disappoint him, and just a little scared of him in general. When he was mad, he yelled. A lot. He was not abusive, but he had a temper. Years later, when I was in college, I learned about the concept of fair fighting, that it was not productive to yell a lot and say hurtful things.

Dad was hardworking, extremely smart, and ambitious. He rose to the executive ranks in his vocation and traveled all over the world. There were large periods of my childhood when I didn't see him much. When he was around, he had an outsized presence, sharing his opinions on a number of topics and making sure we knew his expectations of us. He took good care of us financially, but my mother was far more of a role model to me. Mom was much calmer and was effective at juggling many pursuits. She had a way of putting things in perspective that always helped me see the bigger picture and feel better when things were difficult. Growing up, I had a very particular idea of how I was supposed to act. I don't know if I was born with this, or if I developed it being the youngest child and watching what my parents paid attention to with my siblings, but I craved recognition. I didn't get a lot of that from my father, probably because he wasn't really around. We were not the type of family that said "I love you" or hugged or kissed each other often at all. Dad, in particular, focused on a lot of superlatives. He wanted us kids to be the best, greatest, smartest, etc. He also wanted us to perceive him in these ways, as the smartest, hardest working, and best dad. That was very important to him. Mom was the nurturer and the one with incredible emotional intelligence in addition to her other gifts and talents.

I am the youngest of four children. My brother was the oldest, and being eight years older than me, it almost seemed like he was from a different generation. My two sisters were seven and five years older and were tremendous role models to me. I believe my brother and sisters were probably smarter and more talented in many areas than I was. But, because of how my dad framed success, and since all I ever wanted was to be as good as my siblings, I had an innate desire to be the best at everything. I had to be the best student, best singer, best leader, best—best—best!

I don't know if I was competing mostly with peers my age, my older siblings, or just myself, but I was quite competitive! I wanted to do everything, and I must have driven my mom crazy. Speaking of my mom, once I became a mom myself, I realized just how amazing of a job she did raising us with dad absent for weeks or months at a time. My mother had left college with only a few semesters remaining when she married and had my brother. So, when I was in first grade, my mom, while raising four children largely on her own, went back to college to earn her degree. To this day, I do not know how she was able to juggle all that, but she did it successfully and we never missed a beat. That speaks to the amazing person she is.

How I became so competitive at such an early age, I will never know. I was like a little sponge—taking in everything I was told, and then working to make it so. At a very early age, I would perform "shows" for my family—standing on the fireplace singing or dancing or doing who knows what. My siblings and parents would laugh at me, but they indulged in these attention-seeking activities. I think that may be why I was never afraid to be on stage or speak publicly. When I got into school, I wanted to be the lead in every school play, be the top student, rise to whatever position was the most prestigious. I must have driven my friends crazy! Some of this blind ambition was probably a good thing, as I think it helped me to set high goals for myself. But I also listened to everyone else's idea of what I should aspire to and who I should be. I should get good grades. I should work hard. I should go to college. I should get a good degree and a good job. I should go to church and dress nicely. I should act like a lady, should not smoke, sleep around, or cuss. I should get married, have children, live in a nice home, drive a nice car. Bonus points if I could make it into elite groups like a sorority or The Junior League.

My father was quite opinionated, and even told me which college degrees he would and would not pay for. Funny thing—he did not want me to major in Psychology or Education because he said I wouldn't be able to get a good job and pay the bills with either of those degrees. Now, thirty-three years later, I can say that both of those two fields of study have been instrumental in my career. Although I majored in business (the smartest choice after engineering, according to my dad), I use psychology daily in my role and have spent many years delivering training programs to corporate clients, which sounds a lot like education. Although I was teaching adults, many of the fundamentals of education were the same as if I had been a schoolteacher. I know now that his opinions weren't always right, but it took me a while to untangle his expectations from my own thoughts.

That was my blueprint for a cookie-cutter life. Imagine my shock when I grew up one day and learned that was not how everyone navigated life!

Now imagine my further shock when a therapist, helping guide me through my unexpected and tough divorce, asked, "Why are you so concerned about what everyone else thinks of you?" I was FORTY-FIVE! My life after forty-five has been immeasurably better, because I finally took stock of what made me fulfilled! I hope through writing this book and sharing the lessons I have learned I can help others learn these lessons—easier and earlier than I did. How many women go through life based on what they "should do"?

I learned some powerful lessons from these formative years, some of which I wish I had understood much earlier. For example, while it is great to be desirable, no one else should dictate that for you. And it wasn't until much later that I learned about true significance and the power of self-esteem and believing in yourself, regardless of what people think. My early-life experiences certainly informed the choices I made and the journey that we take as women. I think at times the expectations I placed on myself paralyzed me, and I had a terrible sense of shame when I wasn't able to be the best at everything. I think my journey goes back to the themes of Brené Brown, who reminds us that "you are enough" and urges us to let go of shame and embrace vulnerability.

I had some rebellious moments in my youth, but anytime I did something less than perfect or a bit defiant, I felt a lot of shame and guilt. I was assaulted my freshman year of college, in an all-too-common case of date rape. I would never have gone to the police and prosecuted the guy who did this, because I didn't want the shame of everybody knowing it had happened. I suspect many women feel the same way, and I am dismayed that this happens all too often even to this day. My adult daughter remarked once that sometimes she and her friends would describe a guy as "kind of rape-y," which is so disturbing on many levels. I am glad there are discussions about what consent looks like—and doesn't look like—on college campuses today. This is one aspect of dating culture that really needs to change.

I wanted companionship and safety in my relationships, and I married at twenty-two. It wasn't until age forty-five, after my divorce, when I finally fully unpacked some of the reasons why I chose to take the path I did. It was quite enlightening to uncover why I sought safety, and how much my focus on what I should do impacted my choices.

It is interesting to look back and think about how many things in my life have not gone according to plan, and how much goodness can come from going with the flow—letting go of the pretenses and false expectations about how things should be. Resilience is probably the most important skill I have gained in my life so far. I don't know anyone whose life is picture-perfect, where everything has turned out exactly as it should have been. Those pivots are part of being human—how we learn and how we grow. I think that's a big part of my own journey—of learning to rebalance, to take the good with the bad, learn from that recalibration, and grow.

I was so excited about getting my first "real" job out of college! I had this image in my mind of walking effortlessly in high-heeled pumps down beautiful downtown streets, enjoying my cosmopolitan lifestyle like a cross between Mary Tyler Moore (younger readers, look it up!) and the *Sex and the City* characters. It did not take more than a week or two for me to realize that reality was completely different. It was not necessarily different in a bad way—just different. I quickly acclimated to my new role and enjoyed it most of the time. Immediately I began to watch women who had been with the company longer than I had. How did they carry themselves? What did their career progression look like? And the ever-present question that still vexes me some thirty-plus years later—"How do they balance it all?"

I remember how eye-opening it was to read *The Feminine Mystique*, by Betty Friedan, in a college history course. It was fascinating to learn more about how women showed up in the workplace to help during the war effort in the early 1940s. But then, once the war was over, women were expected to return to the home and give their jobs back to the men who had returned from war. Women were expected to aspire to focus on motherhood, housekeeping, and the home. And yet, women had a lot to give to the workplace. A lot of intellect. A lot of talent. How do we balance fulfilling our needs for love, family, and connection with our need for work, careers, and contribution?

This remains an issue for us after so many years, as we all try to figure out the right balance for our own pursuits, but too often we tear each other down and say negative things about each other. It bothers me when we make sweeping generalizations about our gender. Be mindful before you say something about "all women." I have noticed there are a lot of people out there who try to say if you believe this, you can't believe that. Or we assume that if you look like this, you can't understand that.

Somehow, we have lost the ability to appreciate other viewpoints and agree to disagree. I don't want anyone—male or female—thinking for me or telling me what I should or should not do, be, or support. I can make up my own mind, and I tend to do so with careful thought and consideration. I wonder what would happen if we chose to follow that advice Dr. Stephen Covey suggested in Habit 5 of *The 7 Habits of Highly Effective People*, "Seek first to understand, then to be understood."

—m—

"Besides the noble art of **getting things done**, there is the noble art of **leaving things undone**. The **wisdom** of life consists in the **elimination of non-essentials**."

LIN YUTANG

CHAPTER TWO

What Needs to be *Left* Behind so You Can Live *Right*

As we dive into the archetypes I have observed over the years, it's important to note that any of us may show up anywhere in these archetypes at any given time. To describe these types in detail, we may sound stereotypical. We are aware that not all people face all of these challenges or behave in all the ways described. They are simply meant to paint a typical picture of how this archetype shows up.

The women in our respondent pool, whose names have all been changed, span a wide range of ages, backgrounds, and work experiences, and they were able to readily share stories and insights about each of our seven archetypes. But one of our types brought more than twice as many responses as any of the other six. You might say we were overloaded with examples of the struggles that face **Overloaded Olivia**. A striking percentage of the women we surveyed, particularly the working mothers, spoke expansively about the seemingly impossible juggling act they face—trying to sustain a professional career while still handling an endless parade of parenting and household tasks.

To understand this feeling of overload, look no further than the lists many of our respondents supplied when we asked them about all the roles they play in a typical day. At least one woman could easily name twenty-one different hats she wears either at home or work, and it was quite common for respondents to come up with at least fifteen, citing unique roles like "chaos coordinator," "juggler," "personal shopper," "house manager," "health care administrator," "calendar master," "emotional support human," "math tutor," and "holiday magic maker." If each of these jobs was an actual different hat a woman had to wear, no hall closet could easily hold them all. Add to the sheer number of responsibilities the pressure to do everything well and look cool and collected in the process, and you understand the dilemma of **Overloaded Olivia** perfectly.

This unspoken demand that a woman be all things to all people is, of course, an insidious trap, but the **Olivias** of the world are often organized and capable enough to believe that they truly can keep the balls in the air. The truth is that no one has the capacity to fulfill twenty-plus roles with excellence, though, and each of the women we spoke with has been forced to face that reality. Ellen acknowledges that she has set very high standards for herself at both work and home, standards that are impossible to meet, which leaves her with the need to recalibrate her various roles and what she can pour into each.

Jan, a real estate professional, describes **Olivia's** quandary this way: "We have a huge amount of responsibility on our shoulders combined with a lack of support. We put incredible pressure on ourselves as women to give our all to anything we are attached to—motherhood, marriage, in-laws, community, volunteering, church, and career. So much is expected of women, and women tend to set the bar very high for themselves, which I think leads to a feeling of never doing enough, which can be overwhelming at times." The unhealthy climate Jan describes is even more pronounced in workplaces with unyielding hours and leave policies, companies that make few allowances for the unique needs of the mothers on their payroll.

This perpetual quest for excellence in every realm is a recipe for burn-out, as Celeste confirms, but sometimes women stuck in **Olivia** mode make it worse for themselves by creating impossibly high expectations. Celeste, like most working mothers, has realized that she cannot compartmentalize the different segments of her life in a way that will allow her to focus on work to the exclusion of the needs that she knows will be waiting for her at home. Any working mom who has gone to work and left a sick child knows the feeling of professional responsibilities getting only your divided attention.

"You get up every morning and have to get the kids off to school and then you have to go to work yourself and then come home and try to have your own quality time with them before getting them to bed and collapsing yourself," Celeste said. "So there's just less capacity to give to work. I'm trying to coach myself on this right now, on, 'What is your priority supposed to be? And how can you deliver excellence at work but still be able to do the other things you want to do with your life and take care of yourself too?' You can't just go, go, go constantly. I don't want to say it's all women's fault, but I do think a lot of it is that we want to do it all."

Samantha is tempted to try to have it all, she said, in part because the things on her very crowded plate are all enjoyable and worthwhile. "Saying yes is easy," she said. "Saying no is really difficult, mostly because there is so much that I want to say 'yes' to and yet not enough hours in the day. Balancing everything, with trying to take care of myself and not disappointing anybody, feels like a part-time job on its own."

Amber's daily life often feels like a carnival ride, only not quite as enjoyable, she said, because she is going upside down and traveling at breakneck speed against her will. "When I get on that roller coaster in the morning, it's like I don't get off the roller coaster until the end of the day," she said. "And all of a sudden I'm like, 'Yeah, there are those six phone calls I was meaning to make, to the doctors and other offices that are only open from nine to four.'"

In Alice's opinion, the inability to prioritize, the temptation to hear so many squeaky wheels and try to be the one oiling all of them, chips away at **Overloaded Olivia's** ability to feel fulfilled in her personal or professional life. Every commitment seems equally important, but prioritization is imperative because an **Olivia** cannot possibly invest fully in each one of them. Camille faced a moment of truth in setting priorities when her husband suffered health problems, a situation that prompted her to shelve her professional ambition and focus her attention on caring for him. She has experienced seasons where her work responsibilities took the front seat and other times when family needs came first, but she has become more aware of those shifts, along with the understanding that something will always be getting the best of your time and energy.

Even if our **Overloaded Olivias** find a way to complete tasks at home and at work to their satisfaction, the idea of taking time for themselves, for rest or hobbies, seems like an impossible dream. Maya sums up the world of an **Olivia** this way: "If you succeed at work, are you failing at home? Everyone needs a piece of me, and I end up sacrificing my time or self-care for others. I think women are expected to people please, and when we don't or we say 'no,' we are viewed as selfish or unaccommodating. We also worry about others a lot, making sure all the loose ends are tied up or all schedules are accounted for."

When Heather was starting her career journey in her twenties, she had a dear friend and mentor who had children but still spent hours every weekend at work. Heather vowed back then that she would not make work her top priority to the detriment of her family, and she has stayed true to that promise even if she occasionally wonders about the heights she could reach with a greater commitment to her job. "What has been tough for me has been setting aside my ego, because I don't think I have achieved as much as I could in my career because I haven't always put work as my number-one priority," she said. "I could do more at work, but I've made a conscious decision not to."

As they navigate their overloaded lives, many of our respondents have also gained similar insights about the unique burden women carry regarding work-life balance. So many professional men are fully committed to their families, but they typically have a much easier time putting the concerns of home aside and focusing on their jobs. "I think men have the beautiful blessing from God to be able to turn their brains off," Celeste said. "They just don't carry things the same way that we do. They can just go in and say, 'I'm going to do this,' and then it's over and it doesn't weigh them down when they're trying to sleep." Several other women have also observed this difference, remarking that men seem to have an easier time compartmentalizing home and work. "Women continue to wear all those hats, no matter where they are," Heather said. "The work-life balance isn't truly like a seesaw. It's more like a web."

Anita believes that working mothers find it difficult to detach from the concerns of home because they are conditioned both to be people pleasers and to be the more nurturing parent. Her husband is a surgeon, and she has noticed that he naturally concentrates solely on work when he is at the hospital, and he doesn't feel the pull of home responsibilities. "My husband doesn't care if he never goes to a parent-teacher conference, and he doesn't know where the doctor's office is," she said. "We have very different expectations about things."

I remember talking to one of my male doctors about the differences in the way men and women delineate home and family from work. His wife is a doctor too, so they have equally demanding workloads, but she will text him in between patients with messages like, "Don't forget we have to go buy a mouthpiece today for our son's football game," or other reminders about things going on at home. He told me, "I couldn't believe she was thinking about those things in the middle of her workday." His wife's mental to-do list reflects the fact that **Olivia's** brain is often as overloaded as her schedule.

TRAPS: PITFALLS TO AVOID

Many of the pitfalls surrounding the **Overloaded Olivia** archetype have something in common: Each is a vicious cycle, which both causes the overload issue for working women and is also perpetuated by its ubiquity.

These traps, both cause and effect, are societal pressure on working women, the guilt problem and its connected lack of attention to personal goals, and an inability to pursue professional growth. In addition to all of those factors, an unhealthy byproduct of overloading your life is the physical effect of driving yourself constantly and ignoring the very real necessity of rest.

First, **Overloaded Olivia** falls deeper into the trap of overcommitment because of a professional culture in this country that glorifies the Superwoman image—the notion that a successful woman keeps every ball in the air deftly and does all things well. If a woman who already puts too much pressure on herself buys into this stereotype, she is likely to pile even more expectations on herself to the detriment of herself, her family, and her organization. April attributes some of her own fierce independence to this Superwoman ideal, she said, which conveys the message that she should be able to thrive without help from anyone.

"I have a very supportive partner, but even so I struggle not to feel the weight of all of it on my shoulders," April said. "I don't want to depend on my man for anything—but why not? He's happy to step up. I like knowing that he will, but I hate when I need it. I only want it to be a pleasant option, not a necessity." Sonya says that she regrets "the pressure society puts on us to carry so many different roles and perform them perfectly. We have to be caretakers, friends, confidants, mothers, professionals, and so much more—and we have to give our full capacity to every role. This leads to disparities in the workplace and in society because, when women are unable to achieve this impossible standard that we didn't ask for, we're seen as failures."

Because the expectations many women believe they must live up to are impossible, a companion to the unrelenting pressure hounding an **Overloaded Olivia** is the guilt she feels when she believes she has failed to excel in every area. It becomes an issue of who you are going to disappoint. Will you be late to a family commitment? Or will you disappoint a team member or your boss? You know there isn't enough of you to go around, so you expect to fall short in some area—and to consequently be plagued by guilt. That comparison trap comes into play for **Olivia**; she believes there are other women who are successfully keeping every ball in the air, so when she drops one, she feels guilty and inadequate. I will never forget how discouraged I was potty training my son. I could manage multimillion-dollar budgets and complex projects with ease, but I could not crack the code on potty training!

Joanne describes it this way: "The toughest part of being a working woman and mom is that you feel like you're doing everything but not doing anything 100 percent. There's a constant guilt and pull that comes with having too many responsibilities. When I'm at work, I have mom guilt that my kids are sitting in daycare on a beautiful summer day. When I'm watching my kids run around outside, I feel guilty I'm not spending more time doing continuing education to keep up with my male coworkers. It's a never-ending battle, and it leaves you feeling like Superwoman on the outside and a failure on the inside because you never feel like you're truly focusing and giving your all to one thing."

Joanne's profession in the medical field requires her to engage in continuing education, but many of the courses that are offered compel her to travel and leave her family on weekends or even for an entire week, which is unrealistic for a mother of young children. So she tries to enroll in virtual courses, keeping one Airpod in her ear in the evenings while she is juggling dinner, baths, and bedtime for her kids. She knows that neither her kids nor the class are getting her full attention, but she simply doesn't have the capacity in that moment to devote herself completely to either one.

The third emotional consequence that can afflict **Overloaded Olivia**, along with pressure to fulfill every task well and guilt when that lofty goal proves unreachable, is a fear that pursuing her own goals, or carving out time for herself, is selfish. Selflessness is baked into motherhood; nearly every mother, whether she works outside the home or not, is conditioned to think first about what her child needs and relegate her own wishes to the back of the line. A working mother in **Olivia** mode might have a golden opportunity to gain some new expertise or position herself for a promotion, but if she is overloaded she will probably lack the emotional or physical capacity to pursue that path. Observed Emma, "We're so busy with other people's objectives that we don't create our own."

All these stressors create the real risk of burnout for an **Olivia,** or even health problems connected to unrelenting activity and inattention to personal needs. **Overloaded Olivia** rarely shows up as her best self; she is always in crisis mode, putting out fires because she is carrying too much and can't practically pay attention to each responsibility. If she goes on too long this way, she will find that she can't complete any tasks with excellence because she is merely trying to check items off her lengthy daily to-do list. Healthy sleep, diet, and exercise patterns fall by the wayside, and the joy of fulfillment is dampened at work and home, because both start to feel like a burden.

TECHNIQUES: HOW TO SHOW UP EFFECTIVELY

The way out of the **Overloaded Olivia** trap starts with a realistic assessment of your own values and goals. Women who understand what they treasure the most in life can move from that perception to decisions that will protect those core values. Our respondents, many of whom have traveled down **Olivia's** path and found it unfulfilling, have tremendously valuable insight to offer for anyone burdened by overloaded responsibilities and expectations. Following are some key takeaways for **Olivias** seeking a better way:

Understand that you aren't indispensable and you aren't meant to do everything. Every person has a distinct capacity—for work, for relationships, for tasks on the calendar—and as we grasp our capacity it becomes easier to accept that we all do have limitations. Even if someone at work tries to convince you that things would grind to a halt if you didn't work extended hours, none of us are indispensable, and we can all benefit from accepting that fact and figuring out how to use our limited capacity. Which brings us to the development of that elusive but valuable skill: Saying "no." Some of the people I admire most in my own life are the ones who are comfortable saying "no" and keeping their commitments few and meaningful. As Anya, who listed twenty-two roles that she fills in her life, said, "In hindsight, I wish I had not said yes to everything when I was younger."

Mickie used to believe she had to agree to nearly every request, even if she was being asked to do something outside of her responsibilities or skill set. Then she started saying "no" occasionally, and it was a transformational experience. "Suddenly I got more successful and happier," she said, "when I sort of shed that expectation that I should say 'yes' just because somebody asked. If it was incongruent with even what I like to do, I started to ask, 'Why am I spending even a little bit of time on that?' Let go of the expectation that you have to say 'yes' to everything. if it's important to you, even if it feels like you can't say 'yes' in that moment, you'll figure out how to get to it."

Embracing your capacity and filtering out the commitments in your life that don't fit with your gifts and goals is a vital step toward tearing down the Superwomen facade. Heather had a conversation with an older coworker years ago that has become, for her, a cautionary tale. The woman shared that she had opted to meet with a client out of town and miss her daughter's prom, and she had carried regret over that decision. "There's a misconception in this world that you can have everything, and you know you can have the perfect job, the perfect career, the perfect marriage, the perfect family and you can, and you can have it all right now," Heather said. "But something has to give."

Learn how to set and maintain boundaries. Too few **Olivias** realize that exercising proper boundaries is an essential part of achieving a healthy balance. A key concept of boundary setting is this: We cannot control how others treat us or what they ask of us, but we have absolute control over how we respond to them. This principle allows us to put up borders between our personal and professional lives and respect them, even if supervisors or team members are trying to convince us to violate those boundaries. Several of our respondents spoke about the importance of clear boundaries, acknowledging that as we learn the discipline of setting them we might stumble and cross our own lines initially. "I learned that it's okay not to get everything right the first time," Danielle said. "Failure is not defeat, and I have learned to give myself more grace."

It's easier to keep your personal boundaries in place, Celeste said, when you communicate them clearly to those around you and then hold the line when others try to cross it. Early in a new job, a woman can help prevent becoming an **Olivia** if she tells her coworkers that she doesn't respond to emails at night when she is home with her family, for instance. Or if she tells her team that she is heading to a workout class and she won't be answering texts during that time, she should stay offline for that hour. If she responds to a message in the middle of class, her coworkers are less likely to respect her time going forward. Clear and consistent communication is a truly powerful tool in the battle against becoming overloaded. I have told my superiors, when they ask me to take on a new task, "I can do that for you, but which of these ten things should I take off my plate to make room for it?"

Personal boundaries are just that—individual to each person. One aspect of clear communication in the workplace, as Mickie explains, is helping supervisors understand that each working mother goes about her life differently, and differences in capacity mean that some might be able to comfortably take on more than others. "When I became a mom, people started to make assumptions about what I was willing to do in relation to travel or taking on harder things," she said. "I have had to have many conversations with people who had control over those decisions to say, 'Don't make those decisions for me. Ask me, and I'll make those decisions. I'll let you know if that's not something that that works for me personally, but don't make an assumption.'"

Since Taylor owns her own business, she isn't accountable to anyone else in how she spends her time, but she still must make a deliberate effort to take time away and not slip back into work mode. "I go day and night, but when I shut down and I'm unplugged, I'm gone," she said. "And I know how often I need to do it. And if it means a day, a week, or if it means six weeks of the year, whatever I believe I need for balance, then I take that out of the calendar. So when a client asks for dates, I will say, 'This is when I'm available.' That was something I learned to do early in my career, is to always let people know what I can do, not what I can't do."

Determine your priorities and make decisions with them in mind. This practice, which goes hand-in-hand with boundary setting, requires a periodic assessment of your personal values and goals. Too often Overloaded Olivia is running herself ragged, and she isn't even sure what she's expending all that effort for. I love the way Mary describes this recalibration: "It's exhausting to constantly attempt to live your life based off comparing yourself with what you think society expects of you. You can fall short and feel you're not good enough. You're not a good enough career woman or good enough wife or mother. If women were able to shift their perception or definition of what happiness is, then they might learn how to enjoy the present and be content."

Anita's perception of her daily choices shifted when she stopped compartmentalizing her schedule into work and home tasks, she said, and started viewing each commitment through the lens of what served her priorities. "I think one of the biggest things was embracing that, to me, there is no work and home; there's just your life," she said. "Now I look at the calendar as this is my life, and whatever's on the calendar, it shows what's important to me." In my own journey as a working mother, I have learned to assess the competing demands and make decisions to keep my values aligned with my responsibilities. For instance, I was committed to being involved with my children's school when they were young, so I volunteered to write for the school newsletter or serve as an email liaison between the teachers and the parents, which were tasks I could complete after work hours. I also looked for volunteer activities that would allow me to spend quality time with my kids, such as serving in Scouts and driving Meals on Wheels with them.

Most of our values and priorities stay constant throughout our lives, but even so, it's important to give yourself grace and recognize that life has seasons. Big projects will arise, pulling you away from your family more than you would like, but a woman is in danger of becoming misaligned if she lets those extreme situations become the norm. "Balance is sometimes an elusive concept," said Jess. "Some seasons work wins, and in other seasons family wins. I just try to make sure family wins more than work overall.

"My own expectations of myself and what I can actually accomplish can be a huge barrier personally," Jess continued. "Just because women can do all things doesn't mean I personally have to. Returning to work after having children was extremely difficult for me. My expectation of myself and the standard set by others was that I was going to be able to produce and do just like I did when I was single or married without kids. My own expectations had a huge role to play in this. I addressed the challenge with therapy and trying to set better boundaries."

Stay focused on your legacy. You have heard all the clichés—about how when you are on your deathbed, no one will care how large your paycheck was or how many meetings you attended in a single week. Part of being ambitious is a yearning to leave a legacy. What kind of legacy do you want to leave to your loved ones, your friends, and those whose lives you have the privilege of impacting? I have found it helpful to keep that in mind as I make decisions. Like boundaries and daily priorities, your understanding of your legacy might shift throughout your life, but it boils down to your relationships and the lasting impact you have an opportunity to make.

Grace was reminded of her legacy during a conversation with a close friend, another working mother. Her friend, whose children had been attending school for three years at that point, told Grace that she had never once driven her children to school, because she felt like she had to get to the office early every day. "I said, 'What are you talking about?' She said, 'Well, I'm always in meetings.' And I said, 'Stop right there. Your children are your number-one priority, your job is your job. You need your job. You're going to do your job successfully. But if you're not happy at home, you're not going to be as productive as you could be at work.'"

Just like boundary setting and operating according to your personal priorities, a legacy focus requires **Olivia** to make choices, setting aside something that seems urgent in order to give her energy to the important. As Amber says, "You know all of these stereotypes: that you're supposed to look pretty, and you're supposed to cook, and you're supposed to clean. You know you're supposed to have a beautiful house, and it's supposed to be really well decorated. And you're supposed to be a perfect mother, and la, la, la! But that's where women have to make choices. I don't care if the toilets are clean. I'm spending the afternoon with my kids."

Advocate for your right to be both a mother and an employee. In one of the only benefits of the shutdowns caused by the COVID-19 pandemic, many workplaces have made new allowances for parents to work from home either fully or partially. But still most companies have policies geared toward men whose wives stay at home, and one of the best ways an **Overloaded Olivia** can help relieve her burden is by lobbying for measures that will allow her to continue to complete her work with excellence while maintaining flexibility for the needs of her family. Emily was working full-time on-site for her company when her first child was born, and no one in her department had ever continued the job part-time after starting a family. She wanted to stay, but she knew she needed fewer hours if her work responsibilities and her overall priorities were going to align. So she took action.

"I wrote up a formal proposal as to why I should be allowed to return part-time," she said. "All of the other moms in our department had either quit after their maternity leave ended or come back full-time. To this day, I don't know why they said 'yes,' maybe because I facilitated the workshops no one else could teach or no one else wanted to teach. I learned to speak up and advocate for what I want. It was a win/win!"

Melissa Wirt is a mother of six and the founder and CEO of Latched Mama, a company that makes clothing for nursing mothers. When she created her organization, Wirt was determined to make the culture welcoming for working moms, so she made a policy that employees could bring their babies to work with them and opt for flexible schedules to accommodate children's activities and appointments. Ninety-seven percent of Latched Mama employees are women, and ninety percent have brought their babies to work with them for some period. As Wirt points out, "In twenty-six states it is against the law to separate puppies from their mothers before six weeks of age. That law ensures that companies are not placing profit before the welfare of the animals. Yet one in four human mothers are back at work without their babies within two weeks of childbirth."

The success of Latched Mama has given Wirt a platform to promote more family-friendly policies, and a growing spotlight on parental leave and hybrid work should create more space for women who want to be the best mother—and the best employee—they have the capacity to be.

Surround yourself with a supportive community. It's not unusual for an **Overloaded Olivia** to be so far in the weeds with her overextended life that she doesn't even see the problem, which is one of the reasons supportive family and friends are essential. Your circle, especially those from outside your company, can see when you're walking on the brink and need to set some boundaries or drop some responsibilities. They also love you for who you are, not for what you can provide as an employee or a mother.

I'm so grateful for a group of friends I have been close to for more than twenty-five years; we got to know each other when our kids were all babies. I always made time to play Bunco with them, typically once a month, and celebrate each other's birthdays. Pour into friendships like these—they are so very good for your soul! Some years it was hard to ever make it to Bunco, but I prioritized it whenever possible. Now, years later, we go on girls' trips together, have bridal and baby showers for each other's children, and go out as couples frequently. There is time for this now that our kids are grown. There is a season for everything, but do not wait until you have extra time to sow the seeds and nourish the relationships, because they will sustain you through the tough times! I say that with certainty, as these are the women whose shoulders I cried on during my divorce, who celebrated my new love and eventual marriage to my dream husband, and who showed up at my door with home-cooked meals when I was fighting breast cancer.

And speaking of that dream husband, I must add that a supportive community should start with the person closest to you supporting your personal and career goals, pushing you when your confidence is low, and helping you spot overload. My husband Eric is truly always in my corner, and several of our respondents mentioned their gratitude for husbands who seek to carry some of the burdens that every working mother carries. Tasha experienced a key shift at home when she went back to work, sharing, "My husband stepped up his role as not only provider, but took on more household responsibilities. In addition, and this may be due to their ages, my children realized quickly that I was not at their beck and call anymore. They needed to plan ahead, wait until I could attend to their needs, or problem solve by themselves."

Scarlett's career trajectory has brought about several moves to different cities, and she has been able to pursue new opportunities because her husband fully supported each move and had the flexibility to recreate his business in each new place. She cites an interview with Berkshire Hathaway founder and CEO Warren Buffett, who said in a 2017 documentary about his life that the two greatest turning points in his life were his birth and meeting his first wife, Susie. "What happened with me would not have happened without her," Buffett said. "You want to associate with people who are the kind of person you'd like to be…and the most important person, by far, in that respect is your spouse."

Joanne summarizes our vital need for the right people around us this way: "You can strive for work-life balance, but most days you'll be giving more of yourself to one or the other. It's a constant battle for your time, but if you surround yourself with a strong community—other working women, a supportive spouse, a career that allows you to work in a way that fulfills you—you can "have it all.""

Pay attention to your emotional, spiritual, and physical health. Everyone knows that financial and professional success are only part of the equation, but when **Olivia** is at her most overloaded she is likely to sacrifice the practices that feed her body and soul. Recognize your own symptoms of burnout, and carve out time for exercise, sleep, time with the people you love, and other disciplines that remind you that you are a whole person and not just an employee. Ashley moved from a full-time job into a consulting role, and she marvels at the margin she now has in her life for activities that are life-giving.

"I think the biggest thing I've learned is that it's important to keep your personal happiness in the mix," Ashley said. "Because it's easy enough, at least in my line of work, to just work to be Wendy Workaholic, and let everything else in your life come a distant second. Now that I'm consulting again, I have so much more time to do Book Club and French Club, and pay attention to my husband, and drive my son back into the city, if I want to, on a weekend. Now I kind of scratch my head like, 'Why did I work that hard for so long?'"

—∞—

My Road

As I adjusted to my first job, I was also planning a wedding. I felt a keen sense of what the future held for me as I contemplated marriage, family, and career goals. Being the youngest of four children, I had watched my siblings marry and become parents, and thought that was my expected path as well. I don't think I would have chosen any different path, but it does occur to me now as I look back that I based a lot of my decisions about my path forward on following expected norms. I was destined to become a wife and mother, but also wanted to have a great career, too. It couldn't be that hard, could it?

I forged some wonderful friendships working during those years. I remember meeting one woman who was probably about five years older than me. She was what we called a "high flyer" at the company; she was highly regarded and had moved up quickly. She was also married with young children. She told me she had recently let the company know she wanted to be taken off the fast track. When I asked her why, she said that her four-year-old son had awoken one night crying because he was sick, and he called out for his nanny instead of his mother. My friend said she realized that was not how she wanted her children to grow up.

That story has stuck with me to this day. Like my friend, I knew that was not how I wanted my children to be raised. Little did I know at that time, though, just how difficult it would be to be fully present for my kids and also fulfill all my other roles.

I thoroughly enjoyed my first job. I remember talking with my boss about "paying my dues" to establish my career and get off to a strong start. How you start off with a new company or career makes a big difference in determining the opportunities you can expect to come your way down the road. I worked a lot of hours, took on extra projects, and really dedicated myself to establishing my personal brand. It helped me build a reputation as an employee who loves challenges, is a problem solver, and will roll up her sleeves and get things done—burning the midnight oil to do so.

Ironically, one of the reasons I decided to work my tail off was that one of the more tenured employees who was training me told the boss she wasn't sure I had what it took to excel in the job. And somehow the boss figured out that if you wanted to motivate me, all you had to do was give me a challenge. It was a grueling, non-glamorous job to be sure. I was training to manage a territory of gas stations with convenience stores. It was considered the boot camp for all marketing majors—a ticket to be punched on your way to a bigger, more exciting corporate role. In other words, rather than being that cosmopolitan working woman walking downtown in my beautiful suits and high heels, I was going to wear a striped gas station uniform, learn how to operate a cash register at a convenience store, and manage gas stations. Not only was the product flammable, smelly, and dirty, the job kind of was, too!

Now, to be fair, I had chosen this job knowing I would be doing that. As a marketing major, I interviewed for jobs ranging from driving a potato chip truck, to researching consumer packaged goods, to buying products at market for a department store, to running gas stations. As you might guess, the less glamorous jobs paid better and promised more opportunities for career growth. So I opted to make good money, roll up my sleeves, and manage gas stations. I can confidently say that managing gas stations was one of the best jobs I have ever had, and possibly the best job I could have hoped for. But, at the time, it was the biggest challenge I had ever faced in my life.

Running a territory was like operating a small business. I was responsible for everything—safety incidents, employee issues, hiring/firing, profit/loss, and all aspects of management. What an incredible opportunity for a twenty-two-year-old! It was TOUGH though. These were 24/7/365 businesses before we had mobile technology to make connecting easier. I wore a pager, and many times it rang in the middle of the night when a manager needed to report a robbery, a safety incident, or another emergency. We had fires, prostitution, and drug rings operating out of the stores, and other things I had never been exposed to in my short life.

I spent over a year training for this first job. Being a trainee for over a year was not my idea of fulfillment; I was anxious to get assigned a territory and sink my teeth into my job, but the company was going through a downsizing and things were delayed. Then the big day came—the new organization was unveiled and trainees received the good news about where they would be assigned. My colleagues were all celebrating the news. The only problem was that I heard nothing. And no one could tell me anything. I was not assigned a territory, and I was completely devastated. I will never forget the day in June 1992 when all my fellow trainees got their great news and I did not. We were all at a regional meeting at a local hotel. I went to my car and started making calls. (It wasn't actually my car; it was a company car I was temporarily driving, and it had a car phone. That was a major advancement in technology at the time, and calls were about twenty-five cents a minute during the day!)

Thankfully, no one ever said a word about the hours of calls I made that day. I cried to my husband, my mother, and a few dear friends outside the company. I cried and cried and cried in the car. I thought about resigning, but knew I needed to have another job before quitting. I called a friend who had gone back to school to get her teaching certificate, thinking I might do that. I went home that night, updated my resumé, and started calling friends about prospective jobs the next day. I went in for a few interviews over the next few weeks, but I also showed up for work as usual. I did the bare minimum and tried to lay low while I searched for other employment. I always cared a great deal about what other people thought of me, so despite my embarrassment, I still wanted to show up and be thought of as a good employee. (Again, I did what I was supposed to do!)

Although the other interviews seemed promising, these things can take weeks or months to finalize, and nothing was solidified when, about a month later, I learned why I had not gotten a territory assigned to me like everyone else. The "best" territory was the one with stores in the nice parts of town, which also happened to be where the company executives lived. This territory was the one everyone wanted—not only because the area was nice and the store managers were among the best, but also because it provided a great chance to get visibility to senior company leaders. And if there was one thing we all learned from day one, visibility was ultra-important if you wanted to get promoted, make more money, and build your career. The manager of this wonderful territory, a young woman, had only been in the job about a year, and everyone knew that she wouldn't get promoted that quickly. After all, everything at this huge company was predictable and stratified—until it wasn't. As it turns out, there was an employee being laid off who had a personal issue that affected the timing of the layoff.

So, a month later when this employee was let go, the manager of the amazing territory did get promoted quickly, and guess who got that amazing territory? That's right! ME! Lesson learned—Never assume you know what your career trajectory will be like. My colleague who managed that prime territory was promoted much faster than anyone expected. Good for her for bucking the trend! Also, sometimes there are factors beyond our control that have absolutely nothing to do with us, and if we can just have patience and keep our hope alive, it tends to work out. This is a huge testament to faith, too. Faith is believing in what you cannot see. And I wish I had learned a lot earlier in life that if we truly have faith, the Lord will answer our prayers in ways that may be far beyond and above what we ever thought possible!

"It is literally **impossible** to be a woman... It's too hard! It's too **contradictory** and nobody gives you a medal or says thank you!

AMERICA FERRERA AS GLORIA
IN *BARBIE*.

CHAPTER THREE

Moving Beyond the Impossible Pursuit of Perfection

Think back to the dreaded group projects that cropped up every few months in school. Groups were usually selected by the teacher, and at least one member exerted little or no effort while another person in the group took over the majority of the work, spending exponentially more time on the assignment than anyone else. After carrying the load on so many group projects, that overachiever may have grown up to become **Perfect Paige** when she entered the workplace. As her name reflects, **Paige** is a perfectionist who doesn't tolerate anything less than impeccable preparation and mistake-free work. Because she has such a high capacity to do her job well, in one sense **Paige** would seem to be an ideal employee, but her perfectionistic tendencies limit her potential to grow within the organization and inhibit her value to her team.

Most **Perfect Paiges** have, from a young age, been taught to value their performance above all else. **Paige** may be quite intelligent, ambitious, and capable, but the drive to do it all perfectly supersedes those strengths. **Paige's** belief that she can do things better than others drives her compulsion to do it all. Perfectly. Whether through exhibiting good behavior, earning perfect grades, or developing a flawless extracurricular resumé, **Paige** has received positive reinforcement most of her life whenever she excels. This has convinced her over time that her innate worth is linked to such perfect performance. As she carries these tendencies into adulthood, **Paige** is often a no-brainer in the hiring process, because her resumé reflects her consistent quest for excellence. But the pressure she puts on herself, the skewed expectations she carries, and her fear of true collaboration can prevent her from truly thriving in the workplace.

Researchers seeking to understand the effects of perfectionism on workplace effectiveness have found that perfectionists are more prone to burnout than their coworkers who are more comfortable with making mistakes. One 2016 study, which looked at the dynamics of 437 individuals who worked on teams, found that while healthy perfectionists can bring innovation and excellence to their organizations, those who pursue perfection to an unhealthy degree are often frustrated and unfulfilled. The research also determined that strong friendships on work teams can mitigate the negative effects of perfectionism.

If you are a **Perfect Paige**, you will often approach even routine tasks with outsized expectations. Your most contentious coworker is your inner critic, questioning whether you have done something well enough and raising concerns about your performance that no one around you has even considered. As Lisa observed, "One of the biggest obstacles women face is our own expectations—we expect too much of ourselves and hold ourselves to too high of a standard."

Paul Hewitt, a psychologist who has studied perfectionism for decades, believes that all perfectionism is harmful to some degree, and he draws a distinction between individuals who strive to excel and those who strive to be perfect. The latter, our **Perfect Paige**, is driven by a desire to be accepted, but her constant striving is often linked to a belief that she cannot be "good enough." This can lead to an unhealthy self-perception, stress-inducing work habits, and fractured relationships at work and at home. "Those types of individuals tend not to disclose anything that's going to make them look imperfect," Hewitt said in an article on www.apa.com. "It's difficult to keep them in treatment, because you're asking them to do the thing they've been fighting against."

On the flip side of **Perfect Paige's** need to keep up a flawless image is her intense fear of failure. **Paige** has a hard time accepting or believing in her own success, because every misstep is magnified in her mind. She also may place unrealistic standards on others, straining her relationships in the workplace. True collaboration is impossible when one of the people involved expects perfection at every turn and amplifies the significance of every mistake. A key part of success, in life and work, is persevering through failure and rebounding to try again, and **Paige** can easily get stuck in that process because she can't accept the reality that she ever did a task poorly.

This mixture of sky-high expectations, an inability to handle failure, and low self-image puts **Perfect Paige** at risk for a host of pitfalls in the workplace. Because she shows up as a perfectionist, she may jeopardize her own mental health, distort the reality of her own performance and struggle to build and maintain healthy relationships with teammates and superiors. Next we will look in more detail at some of these traps that could ensnare **Paige** in her relentless quest for perfection.

TRAPS: PITFALLS TO AVOID

One recurring difficulty that a **Perfect Paige** faces in her work relationships is the inability to take criticism when things inevitably don't go perfectly. One or two experiences with even the most constructive criticism can shut her down, shattering her belief in her abilities and sending her into analysis paralysis. With images of the worst-case scenario looming over her, she finds it difficult to complete a task because it might contain an imperfection. In that state of inertia, she disconnects from teammates because she believes that input from others will make the situation even more risky. She might have a hard time meeting deadlines because she always wants to do "one more thing."

Men can certainly fall into the perfectionism trap, but in a workplace traditionally skewed toward male leaders, the temptation for women to function as a **Perfect Paige** is greater. While this is anecdotal information,

I have also noticed that the majority of perfectionists I have come across at work are female. As Annie has observed in her own career, "Women, in my opinion, tend to be detail-oriented and perfectionists. Men generally go with the 80/20 rule and make decisions more quickly." The 80/20 Rule, also known as the Pareto Principle, asserts that twenty percent of a person's efforts are responsible for eighty percent of the results; Annie's experience indicates that men generally try to strategize their efforts according to their strengths, instead of trying to prepare comprehensively and perform perfectly in every area.

Sonya sees a clear imbalance between the expectations placed on men and women in the workplace, so she observes that it's no wonder that women end up tying themselves in knots trying to get everything perfect. Too often, women are programmed to think that mistakes are fatal and success is only possible for the one who has it all together. "Women are expected to be 100 percent at everything they do," she said. "We take small mistakes and magnify them, whereas I believe men blame someone else, make light or joke about it, or downplay their role in it. Men don't let mistakes get in their way of being successful or happy. Women tend to blame themselves or think of reasons how they could or should have done better."

Preparation is one specific aspect of work performance that can be a trap for **Perfect Paige**, the women we surveyed say. The underlying assumption that women have to do more to prove themselves leads them to prepare obsessively for a presentation or a meeting, while their male counterparts might do enough to get by. Mickie was tempted toward perfectionism early in her career, she said, both because she was a woman and because she was younger than most of the other directors at her level in her large international company. She feared that she wouldn't be considered credible enough to offer opinions or make decisions, so she went above and beyond to prove herself. "I had to work really hard to show up prepared with valuable points of view, because what they saw was somebody pretty young, who they probably thought didn't have anything to say or couldn't know better."

Charlene echoes Mickie's opinion about the imbalanced expectation of preparation across genders in the workplace; in her experience, men can approach meetings with a sort of privilege that isn't applied to women on the same team, making perfectionism tough to avoid. "I think women can't just pick up and go to a meeting and sit down and assume they're part of the crowd and everybody's gonna talk through things and be collaborative," she said. "Women have to go into the meeting prepared as though they're somehow in a different group, because they're giving a presentation and want the people at the table to listen to them."

In her 2023 book *The Mirrored Door*, Ellen Taaffe, a professor of management and director of women's leadership programs at the Kellogg School of Management, pinpoints "preparing to perfection" as one of the chief obstacles to women's advancement in the workplace. Women who prepare to a fault will often get praised for it, creating an expectation that overpreparation is the only way, she writes. When they have the right answers, they receive credibility from coworkers and opportunities to collaborate. But this practice can hinder women when they make perfect preparation into a crutch, leading them to work too much and inhibiting them from trusting their leadership instincts honed from hard-won experience.

As Taaffe writes, "Having a reputation of being prepared to perfection is not enough as we aspire to leadership roles. Leaders must be able to decide a course of action with limited information. When we always depend on hours of preparation, we don't learn how to move forward with partial information and the success or failure that results. The well-intentioned, overprepared woman can easily get tagged as great to have on the team but not to lead it. Worse yet, our high standards may make us overly critical of those we are leading and developing. Instead of coaching others to excel, we may fall prey to micromanagement, another perilous reputation."

In addition to the threat of micromanaging teammates that Taaffe points out, **Perfect Paige** is also prone to falling into the comparison trap. On a healthy team people have a range of talents and create a stronger whole from those parts, but if **Paige** thinks she should excel in every area, she may resent others who have gifts that are different than hers. If her confidence in her own ability to do her job is low and she compares herself to those around her, she can fall prey to imposter syndrome, introducing a different type of paralysis. If she fixates on the thought that others are "better" than her and becomes anxious about the reality that perfection is out of reach, she might find herself unable to contribute at all.

As a June 2023 article on insightglobal.com pointed out, one perfectionist on a team can erode unity and hinder every person's performance. "Managers report finding it harder to foster cultures of creativity, empowerment, and personal responsibility alongside overly perfectionist teammates. Individuals imposing excessive perfectionist standards report higher levels of depression due to unrealistic standards, which often snowballs into impacts on the employee's physical health, job performance, burnout/stress levels, and personal relationships," Anna Morelock wrote in "How Perfectionism Can Hurt a Team." Morelock outlined three types of perfectionism: self-oriented perfectionism, other-oriented perfectionism, and socially prescribed perfectionism.

The differences basically boil down to the source of a perfectionist's expectations: Whether they put pressure on themself to be perfect, put pressure on those around them to be perfect, or subscribe to the expectations that they believe society places on them. Those who study workplace dynamics have observed a rise in every type of perfectionism in recent decades, particularly among millennials who have attained positions of leadership. "Studies suggest that globalization, paired with social media exposure, has caused young adults to compare themselves and hold rigid salary, education, and career standards," the article said.

Over the years as I have worked with or coached many **Perfect**

Paiges, I have always tried to talk with them about the fact that they are probably some of the hardest working people in the organization. They are extremely demanding of others because they know what a good job really looks like, and they expect that from other people. Often this is one of the biggest pitfalls for a **Perfect Paige,** because people rarely can live up to such exorbitantly high expectations.

Certainly, **Perfect Paige** does not demand anything of others that she wouldn't be willing to do herself. But therein lies the problem; when **Perfect Paige** fails to recognize that others do not share her capacity, it sets up a recipe for disappointment just about every time. When I use assessments in training, the **Perfect Paige** style often shows up as an independent leader who is comfortable working alone and making unpopular decisions. This need for perfection often leads others to view her as a rather detached leader. While people are prone to respect the work ethic of a **Perfect Paige,** they might get very burned out trying to please her.

I have noticed that often the **Perfect Paiges** I encounter are not big on giving much recognition to their colleagues. **Paige** doesn't typically need superficial recognition, since she is her own constant judge. **Paige** may make mistakes as a leader, though, if she assumes others don't need that reinforcement, or if she avoids it because it's uncomfortable for her. A little recognition goes a long way for **Perfect Paige.** Typically when I discuss these tendencies with a **Perfect Paige,** she acknowledges that her desire to do it all perfectly and do it all now produces nearly constant stress and a lot of overtime. Of all our archetypes explored in this book, **Perfect Paige** puts the most pressure on herself to try to "have it all." If only there were more hours in the day, **Perfect Paige** probably would do it all, but even **Perfect Paiges** have their limits.

TECHNIQUES: HOW TO SHOW UP EFFECTIVELY

Analyze the Root Causes. Women who identify as **Perfect Paige—**

burdened by sky-high expectations and apprehensive of failure—show up in the workplace the way they do because of deeper insecurities or past hurts. To help move out of perfectionistic patterns into a healthy view of herself and others, **Paige** needs to start by recognizing the root cause of her perfectionism. As psychologist Paul Hewitt says, it doesn't do any good to just tell a perfectionist to lower her standards. "I work more on the precursors of perfection—the need to be accepted, to be cared for," said Hewitt, who frequently treats perfectionists. "Those interpersonal needs are what drive the perfectionistic behavior."

Often that process starts by identifying what **Perfect Paige** is believing about herself or others that isn't true. Maybe she has told herself that a project's success is dependent on her alone, or that the other members of her team lack the skills to do their work effectively. Or she might be convinced that one misstep will be catastrophic, when in fact it will merely be an opportunity to learn. Author and psychologist Dr. Robert Leahy, who has written several books addressing perfectionistic tendencies, counsels patients to spend one day doing every task below their usual standard, or imperfectly. This exercise can help prove that perfect is in fact often the enemy of good. "This is what I call 'successful imperfectionism,'" Leahy said in an article on decision-wise.com. "Practicing imperfectionism can help you realize that the world doesn't end when things aren't perfect. It also tells you that you were the only one who was watching."

Grant yourself grace to be imperfect. Perfectionists need to grasp, and believe, the truth that they cannot be good at everything, and that collaborative effort on a team of people with different skills is the best path to successful results. In identifying and honing their own skills and understanding the strengths of their teammates, they can learn to relinquish the burden of carrying the whole group project, the pattern that might have been imprinted on them way back in elementary school. True growth in the workplace, especially for those who aspire to be leaders, means doing fewer tasks yourself and delegating more tasks to people you trust. Micromanaging is a symptom of perfectionism, and its presence on a team erodes the group's unity and limits its effectiveness.

As **Perfect Paige** learns to let go of the impossible standards she has placed on herself and look at teammates, she will come to appreciate their differences, both in ability and in the way they show up and accomplish tasks. Where she might have previously judged her coworkers because they didn't appear to pay enough attention to detail, growth comes when she learns from those who work hard and pursue excellence without falling into perfectionism. We all come to the workplace with our own implicit biases, so a huge step toward showing up better is recognizing those and re-evaluating their source. If you are tempted to think, "That person doesn't work the way I do, so they must be lazy," that impulse is likely springing more from your perfectionistic drive than from true concern about productivity on your team.

Perfect Paige might find that her relationships are hindered by her demands for flawlessness. It is difficult to be close to a perfectionist, especially when she is someone with whom you are trying to collaborate. As **Paige** comes to understand her own motivations and counter her self-lies, she can clear the way to create authentic friendships with coworkers. It has been said that you can't have good foreign relations with others until you have good domestic relations with yourself, and this is especially true for those who are trying to escape the perfection trap and make room for all types at their table.

Like Dr. Leahy and his "imperfectionism practice," a new appreciation of failure and its value can go a long way toward helping **Perfect Paige** develop healthier practices. Of course, just as Paul Hewitt has learned that perfectionists don't respond well to being told, "You should just lower your standards," most people fixated on perfection will struggle with the idea of embracing failure. Those who manage perfectionists can help them see the value of missteps by building a supportive community, highlighting the perfectionist's strengths, and modeling resilience when failure does come. Over time, the repetition of imperfection will allow **Perfect Paige** to loosen her grip on her impossibly high expectations.

Recalibrate expectations. Author Ellen Taaffe points out that women who succeed in their jobs, and subsequently have more opportunities for leadership, can be even more hobbled by perfectionism as they take on new tasks. As they apply their high standards to an ever-widening circle of responsibility both at home and at work, they become even more difficult to maintain. Taaffe encourages her coaching clients to list all the hats they wear and to recalibrate the expectations for each, especially as their obligations increase. This realistic assessment, undertaken with the accountability of mentors and family members, will allow a **Perfect Paige** to see the impossibility of keeping every ball in the air flawlessly. Delegation and boundary setting will become necessities for her to perform at her best in the workplace and remain open to further opportunities.

"So frequently, more is added, and nothing is taken away," Taaffe wrote in her book. "This calls us to operate more efficiently or take things off the list…The paradox is that we can't apply the same level of effort toward perfection that we always have, but we still believe we won't be successful unless we are perfect. To disrupt ourselves, we must rethink perfection and dive into our expectations of the hats we wear."

Paige knows how to work hard and pursue excellence, but if she is driven by perfectionism she is at high risk of burnout and disconnection from others in her organization. As she grows in awareness of her motives, strengthens her relationships with teammates, and approaches her tasks with more measured expectations, she will learn to thrive in the workplace—even when things don't go perfectly.

—∞—

My Road

All of a sudden, I was back in love with my job and my company. I got to stay in Houston, I was managing the best territory, and I had the additional benefit of learning from one of the best bosses I have ever had. Funny thing about that boss—he had previously earned the nickname of "Little Hitler," and a lot of people found him quite tough. I am not at all sure why he earned that nickname or why my experience was so different, but I really loved working for him. Lesson learned—never take things you hear about people too seriously. Take the time to make up your own mind. Rumors generally exaggerate people's negative qualities and originate because the person who started them has an axe to grind. In this case, people who did not work very hard, or who made excuses when things went wrong in their territory, found this boss to be quite difficult. I maintain to this day that those issues speak way more about those employees than about the type of boss he was.

At the time I had this job, twenty-four-year-old me thought it was so stressful! Being on call all the time, managing people who were really different than me, and having so much responsibility made the job tough. But the team I had, the colleagues surrounding me, the boss who mentored me, and the job perks (company car, free gas and insurance, car phone, great pay) made it bearable. In hindsight, I learned so much that would shape my career for decades to come that I cannot overstate the importance of this position. I learned that perspective is critical; everything seems stressful until something more stressful comes along. Employees who have never switched companies think they have it so bad, even if they don't know what bad really is. It's hard to teach that truth, as life tends to teach it to us, but it helps to recognize that things are rarely as bad as they seem.

A week into my territory management job, I learned that a manager I supervised was, as they say, "cooking the books." He was making withdrawals from the store's petty cash account and pocketing the cash. I went to my boss about this, basically to get permission to fire him. This manager happened to be the highest-ranked manager in our area at the time, and my boss asked me a tough question. He asked, "What do you think people will say and think about you if you come in here, a week after getting your territory, and fire our top manager?" I was shocked by that question, and asked right back, "Well, what do you think people will say if they find out that our top-ranked manager was cooking the books and we didn't fire him?"

I was permitted to fire him, and I did. I worried for a while that this guy would hunt me down and find me. He hasn't yet, so I guess I'm okay! A year later there was a scandal in another state where store managers were doing similar things with their petty cash accounts, and many managers, territory managers, and even a district manager were fired in the aftermath. My boss remarked to me that he was happy we had done the right thing with the manager who worked for me, or we all might have been fired. Lesson learned—you will never regret doing what is right, even if you encounter resistance. This is integrity in action; it's so important to have standards and stick to them.

I was just getting good at this job when, about a year after I was assigned to the territory, I was promoted to another role with a larger territory. I was sad to change positions, but I learned another lesson. If you want to have a challenging career and grow quickly, by the time you learn a job, you're probably going to be promoted. That is especially true if you are designated as a high-potential employee. And didn't everyone want to be a hi-po? I sure did. I took every opportunity to volunteer for extra projects, gain visibility, and move toward that coveted hi-po designation.

At Exxon, we were all ranked from top to bottom each year as part of the performance review process. As a new hire, you were inserted into the rankings at the fiftieth percentile unless you were extra special, in which case you would get inserted at the seventieth percentile. I started in June and was too new to do any better than the fiftieth percentile by year's end, so I had a lot of climbing to do to move up. Once I got my territory, I was going to be ranked for real. I was surrounded by peers a lot like me—undergrads from great schools who were smart and capable. We even had a few MBAs or an occasional PhD colleague. It was tough in Houston because it was the headquarters for our company, and a lot of "high-flyers" from HQ would take developmental assignments to "punch their ticket" in the interest of getting a big promotion. People, especially those who think a high IQ is all it takes to succeed in business, are shocked when I tell them I was ranked against these high flyers even though I just had an undergrad degree. And I did ok! Lesson learned—attitude is a huge component of success in business and in life.

In my second role, I worked for a female boss. I thought I would prefer working for a woman, but I can't say that I did. Because this woman was fairly new to managing people, and I was the sole other female on the team, I felt I was treated differently. I should also share that the men who comprised the rest of the team were all old enough to be my father. They took me under their wing, and we had a lot of fun. They had been in the business a long time, loved to party, and I used to joke that I had never felt more peer pressure to party than in that job! They were able to tolerate a lot more liquor than me, and I was always exceedingly worried about how I would drive my company car safely home. So, I learned quickly to nurse club soda with lime and enjoy hanging out with them. These guys told so many funny stories that I could probably fill another book with them.

The boss, however, seemed to expect more of me than the others in the group. She let them be the good ole boys while I was held to a completely different set of expectations. I understood that she managed us differently because I was aspiring to a different career path than them. Sometimes I did wish that the good ole boys would work a bit harder, though, and be held more accountable. This helped me think about how I would manage people differently when given the opportunity.

I made so many memories in this role. I was responsible for negotiating rent with our retailers, many of whom had immigrated from other countries, put all their assets into these stations, and were trying to make a good living to support many family members back home. Being the person who was trying to raise the rent made me the corporate bad cop, and it was quite challenging. I was glad we had fun, or I would have loathed that job. I learned that when the most weaselly retailers ask me to take them to the local strip club, say yes and call their bluff. Thankfully they never took me up on my offer, because I have never been a fan of those places. I also learned a lesson I never forgot—that sometimes the bad guys outlive us. Accepting that some really bad retailers had been there a long time, and would be there long after I was promoted, helped me avoid expending my energy on the injustices of that situation or trying to change anything for the better. That was freeing, although I found it kind of sad to just accept mediocrity.

I learned a great deal about how different the world was than I had previously thought. I was warned not to go to certain parts of Houston after noon, because then the street gangs would be out roaming around and it could be dangerous for me. I learned to relate to people who are really different from me—the cashier earning minimum wage, the immigrant trying to live his version of "the American dream," and people who treated work as a job but not their whole life. Unfortunately, I also gained experience interacting with a few people who were short on integrity and ethics, individuals I was powerless to influence but learned to deal with anyway.

—⁂—

"Cause if I was a man, Then I'd be the man

They'd say I hustled Put in the work

They wouldn't shake their heads and question

how much of this I deserve."

"THE MAN" BY TAYLOR SWIFT

CHAPTER FOUR

Never Let 'Em See You Sweat

Women display a range of protective mechanisms in the workplace depending on their background, disposition, and circumstances. For various reasons—including an introverted personality, past harm in the workplace, or strong boundaries between her personal and professional lives—**Cool Camryn** opts to insulate herself, keeping her head down and getting her work done while limiting her interactions with those around her.

Camryn may typically be known as the office's Ice Princess, the oh-so-calm, cool, and collected individual who presents herself so stoically that coworkers rarely try to break through her tough exterior. She is so guarded that she seldom reveals any of her true feelings or hopes, living by that deodorant motto of "never let them see you sweat." Some **Camryns** are seen as goody-goodys or uppity, declining to participate in joking or gossip and keeping to themselves whenever personal topics are broached in the office. **Camryn** isn't considered relatable, and because she is so reluctant to reveal anything personal about herself to coworkers she often comes off as intimidating and is frequently misunderstood by those around her.

Vanessa, an executive who is an introvert, tends to default toward coolness in her workplace simply because she is a logical numbers-based thinker who approaches problems first from a quantitative perspective, she said. She doesn't discount the more people-based qualitative side of a situation, she said, but she also doesn't lead with emotion or relational factors, and she finds that her approach can cause others to misinterpret her motives. "I tend to lead with, 'Let me figure out what will help me make a really sound business decision and understand the financial implications,'" she said. "And when I feel like we've got that right, I'll pivot to thinking about the people implications."

When other women in her organization lead from more emotional motives, Vanessa has witnessed situations where clear thinking and wise strategy are clouded by an overemphasis on softer factors, she said. Many **Camryns,** like Vanessa, are introverts, and as such they are uneasy about expending too much relational capital in the course of a typical workday. This approach based on facts and logic is sound, in my opinion, and I greatly value it. My personality is somewhat opposite of **Camryn's,** and I have learned that my first inclination is typically to look at the people side of any issue. I appreciate the **Camryns** in my world because I need their perspectives, but I do find **Camryn's** style intimidating. Earlier in my career, I found myself frustrated by this archetype, and I am sure the **Camryns** I encountered were every bit as frustrated by me. Taking time to understand others' personalities is time extremely well spent, and that understanding changed the way I relate to introverts. When a **Cool Camryn** is introverted, I expend more energy to try to effectively relate to her.

Despite the often-healthy emphasis on vulnerability in the workplace in recent years, many women who tend toward **Cool Camryn** are hesitant about the fallout that can come from baring too much of themselves. Celeste has worked under managers who discourage employees from asking for help or sharing authentically, which has had a dampening effect on any instinct she might have to be more honest at work. When the leaders in an organization view vulnerability as weakness, the effect creates more instances of **Cool Camryn**—women who stay in a cocoon and show only enough of themselves to get their work done.

Other **Camryns** come from families guided by an "appearance is everything" ethic, in which sharing too much of yourself or revealing your true feelings about something was viewed as weakness. **Camryns** might also have been conditioned by the voices of mentors who remind them to "stay professional," especially if they have come up through workplaces that did not respect their voices as women. While professionalism is certainly important, too many women conflate the need to project an appropriate image with donning a mask that keeps them at a distance from others.

Taylor said that she struggled early in her career with sharing who she was because she couldn't reconcile vulnerability with the image she needed to project as a leader. "I believe I do a lot to present as a very professional business owner, facilitator, and coach, and I realized that maybe what was missing was me being vulnerable enough to share who I am as a person and who I am as a woman with all those roles in my life," Taylor said. "And I didn't know how to fuse those two together. So I reflected on it, and I took baby steps on what I could do to start sharing."

Like so many of the traps that limit professional women, the tendency to hide behind **Cool Camryn** can arise from an unhealthy workplace culture, one in which employees feel limited in revealing who they are because they have been led to believe that suppressing individuality is the path to success. A 2008 study that surveyed women in thirteen private companies found that women in management roles believe they are under more intense scrutiny than their male counterparts, and this dynamic puts them in a "cultural straitjacket" that forces them into a cool, disaffected persona. "Women become sensitive to their marginality at a senior level and to the lack of cultural accommodation," the study's findings say. "Their visibility renders them highly vulnerable. They display the anxieties of the minority in infiltrating and surviving at the top."

But even if many of the environments that create **Cool Camryns** are unwelcoming and even toxic to women, those who have spent enough time in high-level professional environments know that a certain level of coolness can help fortify women in leadership positions. Brené Brown's work on vulnerability has given us a new language to talk about how we interact with others, but not every workplace scenario is the right place to let down your guard and spill your guts. Leadership coach Christy Rutherford tells a story about a client of hers who overcame great personal hardship to rise to an executive leadership position. Through executive coaching this leader reached a point where she inspired respect from her coworkers, and at one point she told Rutherford that she planned to share her whole personal story at a work event. Rutherford dissuaded her, reminding her that she had done a great deal of work to develop credibility and respect and letting her guard down could do unanticipated harm.

"If you're standing on solid ground mentally, physically, emotionally, and spiritually, and are actively being coached or have a therapist, then vulnerability may be okay," Rutherford wrote in an article called "The Vision Finder: 3 Reasons Women in Leadership Should Not be More Vulnerable": "A strong fortress can withstand most storms, but if you're overwhelmed and exhausted, taking down your guard in an attempt to connect with people who made you create a shield in the first place is not wise."

In my experience, **Cool Camryn** wants to look calm, cool, and collected, and above it all, no matter how stressful it is for her. When someone is more introverted and analytical, people tend to see that person as standoffish, especially if the other person is an extrovert. I once worked with someone who people called the Ice Princess. She was beautiful, as was her spouse. They were like Barbie and Ken. As I got to know her, I learned more about her. She was not trying to be deliberately aloof, but she was not social in the least. I learned there was no need to waste time on pleasantries when working with her. Once I learned to just stick to the facts, we had an excellent working relationship, because we could tell each other what we needed and get great things done.

Like so many of our decisions in and out of the workplace, an understanding of **Cool Camryn** and her suitability for certain situations comes down to motive. Are you hiding your authentic self, and perhaps even inhibiting emotional and interpersonal gifts that could help you thrive, by staying behind a self-imposed shield? Or are you behaving wisely because of proven dynamics in your workplace that make some degree of protection necessary to stay safe and maintain your position? Let's examine the landmines that can await **Camryns** who hide behind their fortresses, recognizing that the process of thawing an Ice Princess should be approached with wisdom and a nuanced understanding of each specific work environment.

TRAPS: PITFALLS TO AVOID

If **Cool Camryn** is burrowing into what she perceives as a safe space, she will likely also isolate herself from others in the organization, leading to a critical lack of connection. If those around her perceive her as superior, judgmental, or even just apathetic about the concerns of coworkers, it makes it impossible to build a fulfilling and productive community. **Camryn** might have impeccable motives, but if she chooses to separate herself from others, she will find that her impact may not match her intent. Relationships will suffer, and she will likely be frequently misunderstood. If she is perceived as unapproachable, people will not feel comfortable approaching her with difficult truths.

There is unquestioned value in setting boundaries at work, but **Camryn** should be mindful not to erect boundaries that are more like unscalable brick walls. She must take care to remain conscious of the value of building relationships, not just to create an enjoyable work environment, but also to meet the company goals. Authentic collaboration is impossible when a leader or team member either fails to solicit input or comes off as if she knows everything already. In these situations, valuable perspectives of people with different backgrounds and insights are completely missed.

I once worked with a **Camryn** who was very composed and did not disclose too much information about herself. She loved working independently and had little need for small talk. She could not stand the ten minutes at the beginning of every meeting where people would chat, because she viewed it as a waste of time. When you are an individual contributor in your role, it's okay to operate that way. However, if you aspire to manage others, you may find it very challenging. You need to get to know your employees and meet their needs to be effective. Not everyone has a 100 percent business approach, and when people can't read your intentions, it can lead to misunderstandings and conflict.

Cool Camryn may come off very calm, cool, and collected, but keeping her guard up can come at a huge personal expense. I have seen women deal with a high degree of stress trying to keep up appearances. I have watched women, in an effort to keep their private lives personal and fully removed from their job, hide things like pregnancies, divorces, and terminal illnesses from everyone at work. That is not in my nature, so it seems a bit sad to me. There are many people who want to be there to support and help their colleagues in times of need, and they are only able to do that if they know what is going on.

Some **Camryns** sequester themselves intentionally, but others don't realize the chilling effect they can have on collaboration or the disconnection others feel from them. Casey tells the story of a CIO in one of the companies she worked for, a capable manager who was hobbled by a disconnect between her intentions and her non-verbal communication. Casey considered her a role model and knew her well enough to see that she was doing herself a disservice and pushing others away. "The way that she held herself, the way that she positioned herself, didn't portray her," she said. "When I see women who have dissonance with who they are and what they really want to be, when you see them outside the workplace, and they're a different person, it drives me crazy. I know we all have to adapt to the workplace, but the strengths they have when we're not at work should be put into the workplace. I don't know why we put on these facades."

Some women stuck in **Camryn** mode stay there because it feels safe, but others make efforts to free themselves from the "facades" Casey mentions and face backlash that sends them back into an insulated posture. Celeste genuinely wants to help create a work environment where others can share their struggles and interact authentically, but she knows that in her workplace such vulnerability has limits. She has expressed herself honestly in the past to a male manager in her firm, and he has not received her transparency as a measure of her commitment to making things better. "He has looked at me like I'm negative, instead of, 'This person wants people to take ownership of their work. This person is realistic and says, 'This is hard, I need help.' I struggle with bringing my whole self to work, because I feel like it's going to harm me."

This reluctance to reveal her true self can be even more pronounced when **Cool Camryns** are women of color, because they have been denied safe spaces in the past and struggle to trust that any organization could embrace them fully. As Toni explains, "Authenticity is a luxury most black women, like myself, indulge with great caution. The perceptions and the judgment are harsh. They can easily lead to termination, withheld promotions, extra responsibilities without pay, and dismissed concerns. To me, work isn't where you make friends. It's where you go to earn money."

Creating an atmosphere of belonging means embracing people from all backgrounds, including those whose differences may not be readily visible. You may work among colleagues who are physically challenged, neuro-diverse, or facing other circumstances you know nothing about. It is one thing to talk about creating a diverse culture and welcoming different perspectives and backgrounds. However, it is quite another to actively display through your behaviors that you truly value this.

A common phrase I hear these days is, "If I can see it, I can be it." When women see other women in leadership, they can more readily visualize themselves ascending to that level. When people of color see other people of color excelling, they see a way to excel and belong at the company. Ask yourself if your company truly welcomes diversity. Do you have different backgrounds, cultures, ideologies, genders, and viewpoints represented? If not, is there a plan to accelerate this path forward for diverse employees? Without attention to representation, it is easy to see why employees like Toni feel they aren't fully safe at work.

Between past offenses, present struggles, and environments that fail to reward vulnerability, it's no wonder that many women stay in **Cool Camryn** mode for their entire careers. But despite a raft of legitimate reasons for staying insulated in the workplace, women and those on their teams will perform at the highest levels and create the most nourishing environments for everyone when they find ways to shed the masks and move forward with warmth, vulnerability, and honesty. That shift requires courage and the examples set by wise women with years of experience either living as or managing **Cool Camryn** types.

TECHNIQUES: HOW TO SHOW UP EFFECTIVELY

Assess Yourself and Seek True Connections. At the heart of escaping the **Cool Camryn** trap is the simple, yet often incredibly difficult, principle of showing up in the workplace as yourself—willing to engage with vulnerability and make true connections with others. The starting point for any move in that direction is to make sure your organization is a safe place to live authentically. But even in a healthy work environment, the shift from a cocoon to a wide-open space requires intentional steps, starting with humility.

What does humility look like in your work interactions? It's a willingness to do an honest self-examination about how you come off to coworkers, clients, and managers. It's a readiness to accept the leadership of others even if they don't always operate the same way you would. It's even the inclination to let your hair down from time to time, when the circumstances allow it. Recognize the importance of interaction with people just to get to know them and connect, rather than always seeking a business objective from every conversation. Seek opportunities to laugh, share the things you love outside of work, and learn what makes others tick. To be sure, showing up with humility brings risk, but the potential benefits—in deeper relationships, more cohesive teams, and more mission-driven organizations—are vast.

For leaders, showing up with humility looks like the acknowledgement that leadership is followership. Put another way, leaders who want to engage the people on their teams authentically and break down the **Cool Camryn** walls need to understand the motives, needs, and goals of those who are following them. Jim Kouzes, renowned leadership expert and author of several best-selling books including *The Leadership Challenge*, reminds us, "If you think you're a leader and you turn around and no one is following you, then you're simply out for a walk." Just because your name is above someone's on an office flow chart doesn't mean that you have displayed the humility and intentionality to truly be deserving of a following.

Consultant and author Patrick Lencioni tells the story of an early consulting client, a well-known CEO who seldom gave feedback or tolerated disagreement from the people who worked for him. At the urging of his human resources director, the CEO eventually agreed to undergo a 360-degree evaluation, but then only shared the results reluctantly when the HR director urged him to. He called a staff meeting and then confronted the employees with questions like, "It says here I'm not a very good listener. What do you guys think?" "It says I don't give enough praise; do you think that's true?" In that high-pressure environment, no one owned up to any criticism of the boss, giving him only praise, until

Lencioni interjected to point out that the people in the room had filled out the 360 survey, so someone must have feedback. Despite Lencioni's efforts, the CEO never admitted to any of the weaknesses revealed in the survey, and several years later his company was sold at a significant loss.

"All he had to do was say, "Guys, I know I'm not great at these things. I'll try to get better,'" Lencioni said. "There was no trust on the executive team, because the leader of the company couldn't say, 'I'm wrong. I need help.' If the leader cannot be vulnerable, other people are not going to be able to do that."

Proactively Seek Conflict Resolution. Too often **Camryns** fall into passive-aggressive behavior, because to engage in conflict is to unleash emotions that they have hidden away. They studiously avoid confrontation until they can no longer bear a tense situation, and when they finally do speak out, the pressure has built up so much that they erupt, bringing more emotion to a situation than it actually warrants.

Sidestepping the opportunities to address problems appropriately also tends to cede the floor to hotheads and attention-seekers who have an opinion about everything. When those individuals suck the air out of the room, the **Camryns** who have something valuable to share lose their opportunities and erode their relationship collateral. To combat those unhealthy dynamics, **Camryns** have to find the boldness to address issues and questions in a timely and appropriate manner rather than letting problems fester and grow.

Devote Time to Building Relationships. It is true that some **Camryns** are genuinely introverted, and expending themselves with humility, vulnerability, and boldness will deplete their energy supply more than it would drain others. If shedding the **Cool Camryn** cocoon is tied to authenticity, an introvert should bring that aspect of herself to the table as well, acknowledging her limitations but then making the effort to show up for those around herself anyway. Whatever our natural social characteristics are, connecting with those beside, above, and below us is essential to functioning well as a team.

Early in her career as a business owner, facilitator, and coach, Taylor was so focused on presenting a professional image that she often missed opportunities to share who she was with those in her workplace orbit. As she came to see this disconnect and resolved to build a bridge between her "real-life" self and her work self, she took those baby steps to start sharing examples and stories from her family life and hobbies. "I would give examples, and I would, bit by bit, start sharing who I am," she said. "I noticed even when I was meeting with potential clients, I would share and be authentic about who I am and what my role is, or something about my family or some things that I like to do personally. And I found that it strengthened the connection immensely."

As she becomes more comfortable showing up authentically, Taylor has seen those around her shed their masks as well, she said, especially women who are learning that prioritizing relationships makes work not only more enjoyable, but also more fruitful. She has come to value this quality so highly, she said, that it comes into play when she is seeking new employees or considering new client relationships. It's no different than when people say, 'Hire attitude first and we know we can train them,'" she said. "I feel the same way about being authentic. I think it is really, really important. I want to know my clients, I want to know the people I'm working with, but I need to be able to share who I am to give them a safe space to do that."

Taylor's burgeoning belief in the power of authenticity, and the importance of modeling that genuine approach to others, outlines a practical answer to the crucial question, "How does a manager help lead a **Cool Camryn** who seems determined to stay hidden?" Taylor might have started her move to authenticity with baby steps, but over time she has helped lend courage to other women who see the freedom offered by her more expansive way of showing up. If you have one or more employees who insulate themselves as **Camryns,** you can draw them out by modeling authenticity and by taking the time to understand the wounds that sent them underground in the first place.

Throughout my own career journey, a common characteristic shared by all my best bosses has been a desire to truly know their employees— their backgrounds, their needs, their struggles, and their dreams. Leaders who customize their style of management to each person under their management have a far greater impact than those who adopt a cookie-cutter style. Ultimately, if an organization's culture invites authenticity and its leaders lean into that value every day, the **Cool Camryns** will see a navigable path to freedom from their self-constructed barriers. And if you do not feel you can show up to be yourself and be valued authentically for your contributions, you may be in the wrong role or at the wrong company.

—m—

My Road

About a year into my second Exxon role managing gas station retailers, I had an unexpected transition to a new job due to a health issue. I had been diagnosed with keratoconus, an eye disease that made my corneas cone-shaped, at twenty-two. Most people who have this disease manage it with contact lenses and never have major issues, but it turns out I was not like most people. Within the space of four years, I went from starting to wear glasses to needing a cornea transplant. The disease had progressed; I was legally blind in one eye and it could not be corrected with contact lenses. The surgery went well, but the recovery was pretty awful. I had stitches in my eye for about five months, which were removed one or two at a time every few weeks, with one running suture staying in my eye for two years. I wore a patch several times a day until the main stitches were out.

The first transplant was a great success. My second transplant occurred about ten years after the first one. Once again, the recovery from surgery was long and unpleasant. This time it was a bit easier, though, since I knew what to expect. So, thanks to the miracles of modern medicine, I was able to avoid blindness. I was left with poor depth perception and still wore contact lenses, but my vision was close to 20/20 for many years.

Exxon was great about accommodating my situation during this time. Because I could not easily drive the 3,500 miles a month it took to cover my large territory, they moved me to a reorganization team in the headquarters building downtown. This was a great opportunity for me, although it felt like a setback when I had to buy a car, purchase car insurance and gasoline, and get my own mobile phone. (Yes, I called my phone that was heavier than a brick and about as large as my laptop a mobile phone.)

Nevertheless, I was downtown, a step closer to that *Sex and the City* dream role. I even wore suits! With high heels! And walked down the city streets in those shoes. About twice, until I realized how much pain I was in! I had visibility, a role in improving our field processes, and a place on a great team. I also, unfortunately, had one of those not-so-great bosses. Why was he bad? Now that I have the benefit of hindsight, I know it was that I did not know how to relate to him. He was a harsh critic and had very high expectations. He wanted to see my final drafts, not rough drafts, and was not much of a conversationalist. I figured out the hard way that he appreciated my weighing my words very carefully. I grew to respect him immensely once I figured out how to work with him. A few years later, he paid me a compliment that showed me he respected my work as well. I learned a great deal from him. Lesson learned—sometimes the toughest bosses can teach you the most if you are open to learning.

After assuming this role and undergoing successful eye surgery, I was assigned to one of the best teams at headquarters. I worked on a top team for one of the "greats," working to develop a new credit card. What a job! I got to travel, negotiate contracts, and enjoy a position that had great visibility. I had a boss who took wonderful care of me, finally getting me to the coveted top ten percent of the rank group, labeling me as a hi-po. Why was that so important to me? Although I should have known better, now I know I was defining my success by what others thought about me and by what others thought I needed to achieve to be successful. To be fair, though, it is easy to do that in a job. After all, when other people think you are doing a terrific job, you tend to make more money, get promoted, and receive other perks. And as I said, I still cared a great deal about being my best.

At that time, being my best correlated well with how the company defined the best. I know now that is not always the case. My boss was quite interesting—phenomenal in many ways and frustrating in others. (Lesson learned—this is typical of most leaders!) He had faith in my abilities, probably more than he should have. He wasn't around a lot since he kept a grueling travel schedule. He gave very little direction and provided me plenty of autonomy to figure things out. However, this was difficult to navigate, since I didn't know what I didn't know. I found it frustrating to constantly have to figure things out the hard way, although I suppose I did a decent job of doing so.

I worked quite hard and made great progress, but I found myself getting burned out. Also, my husband and I were trying to start a family and it was not going as planned. I don't know whether being down about not getting pregnant made the job worse or whether it was just the stress of having a very demanding job. A few things became evident to me: first, to maintain hi-po status I would need to continue working at a breakneck pace, which could be in major conflict with my motherhood philosophy of being present for my future kids. And second, I did not want to move to another part of the country for my job since my husband had a great job in Houston and my family was there. I was really frustrated because I wanted to have a baby, but we had some fertility issues.

Finally, my husband told me not to sit around waiting to get pregnant. He said if I wanted to make a job change, then just do it. So I did. Eventually. But first, I mustered up the courage to talk with my boss and tell him what I wanted. At that point I had resolved that if I received a negative reaction from him, I would be prepared to quit. It is unfortunate that having a candid conversation with the boss felt like such a huge risk. I then understood just how terrifying it could be for an employee to have a high-stakes conversation with their superiors. And that is a real shame.

I took a leap one day and told my boss what I wanted—to move into learning and development for my next role, not to some analytical assignment in a new town. He laughed, saying the company already knew I was good at training, so I needed to display my analytical skills to check that box for promotion. In other words, what I wanted did not factor into the equation. That very day I made a call to a company where my friend worked and began searching for a full-time role outside Exxon in learning and development. A month later I received an offer from that company and I quit my job at Exxon. I don't know who was more shocked—me or my boss. I was told, "But we have plans for you!"

I realized the promise of a wonderful retirement in twenty-five years, if it meant relying on someone else to raise my children, was not going to work for me. Lesson learned—don't define your career path based on those who have come before you. Make your own unique path. Exxon was an amazing training ground, and what I learned there has helped me for decades. However, I am thankful I did not let the promise of a bright future there keep me from jumping ship. This was the beginning of living my life—or at least my work life—on my own terms.

—⁓—

"The road to success is always under construction."

LILY TOMLIN

CHAPTER FIVE

The Cost of Toppling Barriers

Any adventure movie enthusiast can tell you that heroism comes at a cost. Picture an intrepid Marvel character or college-archaeology-professor-turned-jungle-crusader after conquering whatever dark forces opposed them, and they are inevitably bruised and dirty, and sometimes even limping or scarred. It might not be as dramatic as saving the galaxy from Thanos or preserving the Ark of the Covenant, but knocking over workplace barriers and making the way smoother for the women who will come after can leave scars of a different type. And in the middle of those battles, making her own narrow escapes even as she leaves a better world in her wake, is **Trailblazer Tess**.

Some **Tesses** have blazed a trail through predominantly male workplaces, while others are women of color putting down stakes in a corporate world where they are woefully underrepresented. Their early careers might have been a study in risk-taking, especially since conventional wisdom said that they should not attempt to succeed in an environment where so few people at the top look like them. They are often determined and strong individuals who have persevered through stereotypes, lost or stolen opportunities, and possibly even sexual or racial harassment or abuse.

Wearied by these battles, **Tess** might choose to close herself off to connection or advancement, because previous attempts have ended too painfully. She enters the workplace wearing armor, withdrawing into self-protective mode. Younger **Tesses** might have been belittled or harassed during their college years or early in their careers, confirming their fear that they don't really have what it takes to succeed in the corporate world. Before she was battered by bad experiences, **Tess** approached her job with the kind of optimism, courage, and relatability that can bring long-term change to an organization, but the landmines she has encountered can wreak havoc on those qualities and send them underground.

Karla is a college professor teaching and researching in the world of sports studies, working to show up authentically when both facets of her field, academia and sports, are dominated by men. She is a strong woman who is not afraid to speak out and lead, but as she pioneers in new spaces she said she has been impacted by the reactions of others. "I think a lot of men do not realize the internal challenges that women face to find a balance," she said. "A strong woman is a bitch, while a kind and compassionate woman is a pushover. Trying to find and actually have to think about that balance is something that women have to approach differently than men do at work. I'm constantly told I'm intimidating, and I think that has impacted my confidence with relationships outside of work."

Maya is another inherently strong leader who has had to contend with misperceptions in her workplace. In her early years she wrestled with imposter syndrome, wondering whether she would actually be permitted to show up as her true self and succeed. "I've always had to prove myself, my worth, my contribution, and my knowledge," she said. "I think sometimes, men come to the table already respected and equipped with authority, like it's automatically assumed that the men will succeed, whereas women come to the table expected to fail and to not have the authority or respect we deserve." Those unhealthy patterns, carved through years of mistaken perceptions toward professional women, can prevent those who identify with **Tess** from thriving and recognizing their importance to their organizations.

Like Maya, Katelyn repeatedly feels the need to prove she belongs in spaces, even when she has already done the work to earn her position there. It feels like a vicious cycle, she said—go above and beyond to prove your worth, finally become comfortable, then work for a promotion and realize that you have to pass that same women's-only test to gain credibility at the higher level. "It's constantly just that cycle of like, 'Oh my gosh! Now I have to prove myself over and over again, even though I've been vetted out by a ton of people to get here,'" she said. Sometimes men who are threatened by strong women and may believe they have an upper hand can sabotage female coworkers or subordinates, rendering them unable to operate to the best of their abilities because their efforts aren't appreciated or rewarded.

For women who manage men, the remarks and attitudes driven by gender bias and disrespect can feel like death by a thousand cuts, attempts to erode a woman's credibility and authority. Sally has experienced this in her work as an executive coach, as men have made comments to her like, "Could you speak up? I always have trouble listening to a woman's voice," or, "I forgot what you just said, could you repeat it?" These attempts to belittle Sally, to suggest that her voice is not worth being aired, illustrate vividly why **Tess** often limps through her workdays. "There were times when I had men telling me how hilarious they thought it was to create a problem and then watch how I would solve it, also sharing that it is always funny watching women running around, 'doing woman's work,'" she said. "I asked one of the men what this meant, and his face turned red and he walked away."

In some professions, women can be trapped in a **Tess** persona because of gender stereotypes held by their customers, who might think women cannot excel in certain roles. One of the two dentists we interviewed, Wendy, said she is often made to feel less capable because people don't "expect" a woman when she walks into the room. On one occasion she was almost finished filling a man's cavity when he stopped her and asked, "When is the dentist going to come in?" She said she has been asked "at least a hundred times" if she is the hygienist, and even though she trusts her training and expertise, she can't help but be affected by the doubters at times.

Let me be clear: not all men treat women poorly in the workplace. Quite the contrary – some in our research mentioned male colleagues as tremendous allies, mentors, and lifelong friends. Those men who do behave badly toward **Tess** are not the only threats she faces. In fact, the biggest threat to **Tess** may be fellow women. It pains me to say this, but there are women who treat other women terribly. The reasons for this may be quite complex, and unpacking their motivations may prove quite challenging. I have seen women show up at work exceptionally competitive and driven, out to prove something to the world. Others are fueled by a scarcity mentality, which makes them feel threatened by other women. Regardless of their motivations, this is a sad byproduct of the success women have worked very hard to achieve.

Whether **Tess** has been muted by higher-ups, reduced by the perception that women are only valued for their looks, or overtly harassed due to her gender or race, **Tess** has become so caught up in the need to survive a hostile environment that she has lost sight of who she is. The unhealthy journey toward becoming stuck in **Tess's** traps typically starts when young women entering the workplace feel compelled to legitimize their presence and make their voices heard. Those early patterns are forged by managers who fail to develop their female employees and those who perpetuate hostile or oppressive work environments. I have seen women who come into a new position with excitement wither when they aren't valued. Soon they are trying to emulate others in negotiating the workplace, leaving their own unique talents by the wayside because they figure that is the only way to get results.

Everyone around **Tess** is missing the chance to know and work with her in an authentic manner because she has donned her coat of armor to protect her from more pitfalls along her journey. Sadly, this leaves **Tess** unable to relate well to others or celebrate her triumphs.

TRAPS: PITFALLS TO AVOID

Now that we have a clearer picture of what characterizes **Tess**, the next step is to understand the thorny traps that can hinder her vulnerability and growth. Many of the women I surveyed shared that the toxicity of a current or former workplace forced them to either adapt in unhealthy ways or leave a job. There is nothing sadder, from a professional perspective, than seeing a bright, motivated young female employee become worn down by power plays, outright sexism, and disparagement of a poisonous work environment. Subjected to this, **Tess** often falls into one of two traps— into a persona that makes her act more like a man or into a subservient wallflower who no longer uses her voice to make a difference.

Linda, an engineer, has seen every manner of **Tess** pitfall throughout her career, from men judging female job candidates by their attractiveness to a client using verbal threats to intimidate her. But even though she is no stranger to men behaving badly in the workplace, Linda's most difficult boss was a woman who had clearly resolved that the best defense against mistreatment was to become as tough and unapproachable as possible. This technique might have provided the boss some protection, but it made connecting with her difficult and ultimately made her ineffective as a team builder.

Before I decided to leave Exxon, I spent a lot of time looking around at the women who were excelling in my workplace. I had just worked my way into the top part of the rank group, which apparently meant that I had a good career ahead of me, but I noticed that most of the women who were getting promoted either had stay-at-home husbands or husbands who also worked for the company. I also noticed that the women who were really excelling were the ones who were acting like men.

There was one woman that everybody said was a high flyer; she had quickly moved up into a key leadership role. I heard stories about how she had a baby and was back at work the next week, despite having six weeks of maternity leave. She also allegedly found a way to fly at nine months pregnant, because she couldn't bear to miss a trip for work. She set a precedent that I don't believe helped the rest of us who wanted to have some work-life balance. When I announced my resignation, my exit interview was set up with that woman, and I asked my boss if I could have my interview with someone different because I didn't think my concerns would land well with her.

Even if they aren't purposefully trying to join the "boys club," women in male-dominated workplaces are faced with a barrage of choices that have little to do with their professional performance, like whether to join activities organized by men, how much to participate in certain types of joking, and what to wear and how to accessorize. Several of the women in my survey group said that they had been on work trips in which men conducted business at strip clubs, forcing them to decide if they would go along for the sake of the team or the deal or stay home. I was in this situation myself, when at twenty-five years old my gas station retailers asked me to take them to a strip club for a work meeting. I told them sure, I would be happy to take them there. Thankfully, they never took me up on that! I think they were completely shocked that I agreed to do it and were simply trying to see my reaction to their invitation. Anita is an accountant who sees receipts from strip club outings come across her desk, and when she declines the reimbursement, the manager in question is quick to call her and argue the legitimacy of his "business expense."

It might seem minor to someone who doesn't work in the corporate world, but for many professional women the question of attire consumes far too much of their attention, either because the men in their organization focus on it excessively or because suitable dress standards, and the reasons for those, have not been communicated to them. Laura summed up the double standard embedded in the challenge of dressing for success when she said, "Women can be oversexualized in the workplace if they're looking too nice but also steamrolled over for not looking good enough. Looks seem to matter more for women. Men just need to shower and put on a decent suit." Quinn, who works in politics, adds, "You can't win. If you're tall and you wear the same dress as a short woman, you're showing too much leg. If you wear pants you're too masculine, if you wear bright colors you're a fashionista, if you wear muted colors you look like you want to be in the background. Everything gets a response, and everything is scrutinized."

The respondent pool agrees that expectations for what women should wear to work have thankfully loosened over the past few decades, as older working women still remember when the only "appropriate" choice was a boxy black suit with pantyhose. Stephanie, an executive in the oil and gas industry, remembers a time early in her career when a supervisor told her that the senior manager "likes his females to wear skirts." It was ninety-plus degrees in the summer, and Stephanie's job at that point was to visit gas stations all over the city. Ashley is an attorney who can trace many of her early-career insecurities to the wardrobe that she felt was forced upon her. "Coming out of law school, I wore that silly stewardess-like navy blue suit with the white shirt and the bow tie," she said. "What's up with that? I actually wore that for two years until I realized I could wear what I'd like to wear."

Today Ashley wears a lot of pink to the office, she said, and she has discovered that authenticity in her clothing choices leads her to show up at work more genuinely. But like others who have been in the workplace for years and have seen different attitudes among younger women, she still believes that professional standards serve a vital purpose in maintaining the right type of atmosphere. "There's a balancing act," she said. "Now what I worry about with younger women is that they think they have a right to be their authentic self, no matter what that means. So if they feel like wearing a black lace bustier to the office, they think they can do that. You have to know the boundaries."

Anita remembers when a bright and promising young accountant came to the office one day wearing bright yellow stockings with a tattoo design printed on them. Anita asked her about her clothing choice, especially since an executive vice president, someone with the power to boost the young woman's career, was coming for a visit that day. "I asked her, 'Do you think he's not going to judge you? Because I guarantee you that he is going to judge you. I try so hard to promote you. and it's not a hard thing to do, because you're super bright and you're super talented at what you do. But you cannot sabotage yourself with idiot choices like this.'" The young woman was momentarily shocked by Anita's frankness, but then she said, "Well, I guess I should go home and change." Anita was able to teach the younger employee that despite the unfair scrutiny women face, some guidelines exist for the right reasons and should be adhered to.

The particulars of that balancing act Ashley described are tricky, and they vary from workplace to workplace. It took years for April to feel confident enough to come to work with a non-traditional hair color or fashions that aligned more closely with her personality, she said. Initially she thought she had to keep some of her "true self under wraps," she said, but eventually she became a little bolder in her choices and was promptly shut down by a trusted mentor. "I was very directly told that my look would hold me back," she said. "My response was, 'What a shame my efforts and exceptional experience have less to do with my potential than my hair color.' It was disappointing, to say the least."

Terri was a literal trailblazer in a STEM profession, and she has noticed that some women in her field handle being outnumbered by trying to become "one of the guys," an approach that nearly always backfires. "I think sometimes they try to take on a male persona and it's a very aggressive and demanding persona," she said. "I think we need to embrace our feminine side and still be strong."

Whether or not **Tess** has found herself diminished by power plays, petty criticisms, or struggles with standards of appearance, she is likely to be tempted to become less than herself as a defense mechanism. In the early days of Quinn's career, she was inhibited from seeking a promotion because imposter syndrome had made her doubt the value of her contributions. When she marshaled the courage to approach her boss, she was given the promotion. "I wish I had insisted on the promotion sooner and not been so timid," she said. "I realize now that my being timid and doubtful gave them reason to believe they should perhaps doubt me if I doubted myself, which slowed the process."

TECHNIQUES: HOW TO SHOW UP EFFECTIVELY

For **Tess**, whose *modus operandi* is to blaze her way through the workplace scarred from previous battles and armed with the weapons she believes she needs to survive, the first secret to showing up authentically is to imagine a different way. Often she has built up her armor, embattled from too much time operating in unsafe environments, and accessing the self-awareness to emerge from that protective shell will require courage and vision. Some key strategies for a **Tess** include:

Show yourself some R-E-S-P-E-C-T and show up to earn the respect of others. The way out of the **Tess** trap, or the path to avoiding its clutches in the first place, starts with authenticity and self-respect. Knowing the unique talents and skills you bring to a team and recognizing the role of emotions in the workplace enables women to bring out the best in themselves and those around them without compromising. This shift might seem overwhelming, but it starts with small changes. Believing that and acting the part goes a long way toward creating an environment of mutual respect. Know the difference between being respectable and actually earning respect. We might believe we are respectable (and hopefully we are!), but building respect is an active process. Respect is earned or taken away in every interaction we have. Considering how you show up will go a long way toward becoming the type of leader people want to follow instead of being a **Tess** who alienates people around her.

Think about how you want to be perceived—what you want people to say about your communication style and your contributions. Then take steps to prepare for conversations so you are ready to show up that way. This is different than pretending to be someone else. It is about being the best version of yourself. It may feel a bit like pretending at first, but as you practice showing up purposefully it will become far more natural.

Resist the urge to overpower or retreat. Be the change you want to see: If **Tess** has been shut down repeatedly, she has often developed such a tough exterior that she shares few ideas and even fewer genuine opinions. The key to forging healthy and productive communication patterns is resolving that her voice is vital to the success of her team, and then using it to send strong messages with subtlety and grace. A woman who has been wounded by toxic power dynamics must resist the urge to overpower the ones abusing their power, while also keeping herself from retreating into hiding. That is, admittedly, a difficult balance, but it is possible to stand strong with authenticity and a commitment to true collaboration.

Not long ago Linda was subjected to verbal threats from a client who challenged a decision she made, but the incident didn't devolve into a retreat situation for her because she knew she was in the right, so she stood her ground politely but firmly. She knew that her management had her back, so she made her case confidently and moved on from the incident.

Having started my first company at twenty-nine, I was younger than most entrepreneurs, especially women in my industry. I always felt like I had to prove my worth and my intellect. It took me a long time to realize that when I exhibited confidence and spoke in an engaging manner, choosing my words judiciously, people would listen. The higher I rose in an organization, the less persuasive and passionate my message needed to be. I had earned the right to be there, and others respected my viewpoints.

I wish I had learned this earlier. I think I wasted a lot of time and created unnecessary personal stress selling my ideas and justifying my views more than needed. There are certain things women say that diminish our credibility in an instant. We might apologize too much ("I'm sorry to bother you…") or minimize our authority by saying the word 'just' ("I just want to talk with you about…"), and then wonder why we are not treated with respect. This is a time when we should take a page out of our male counterparts' book. Do you hear them apologize for wanting to talk with you, or minimizing their requests by adding a "just" in there? I'm guessing not.

Handle differences with tact and finesse. A **Tess** who is committed to shedding her defenses will ask good questions, hear every point of view, and help teammates find their own way to the conclusion she has already reached. She will resist the urge to confront, instead inviting the possibility for a productive conversation. When differences cannot be resolved, she will continue to interact with grace and generosity, clarifying out the divergences of opinion but never making things personal. A woman who has been attacked or taken advantage of in the workplace can become the most sensitive and consistent advocate for building an environment that refuses to accommodate such behavior in the future.

One of the best things I learned from my last boss, who was a very influential executive with a large company, was that the more influence you have—and the more power you have simply by virtue of your position and credibility that you've earned—the less heated you need to become about your points of view. Watching the finesse with which she handled situations where she needed to share a dissenting opinion or steer things in a different direction taught me an incredible amount. I think up until that point I was so busy trying to prove myself to the world that I felt like I had to really assert my position in work situations. Learning that I could simply state my opinion calmly, and be confident that it would be considered, was huge for me.

Channel emotions effectively. Women who have armed themselves with **Tess** tendencies have perhaps been told, "You're too emotional," or maybe they did give into excessive emotion in a work setting and found it difficult to reclaim respect. Emotion is too often thrown out as a negative, when some of the most effective professional women know that emotion is a valuable tool when used correctly. Women in the workplace don't have to lock their emotions away, but leading with them is unreliable.

Instead, pay attention to the presence of strong emotions while refusing to let them in the driver's seat. Read the room first and speak in a way that can lower the temperature when things might feel ready to ignite because of anger and discord. Executives value, and employees follow, those who lead in rationality informed by emotions, rather than impulses dominated by them. As one executive, Samantha, stated, "I think one of the superpowers of women is that we bring vulnerability into the workplace in a way that men tend not to. I also think that we tend to lead with the heart, which can be very powerful."

Deal with your stuff. Own your stuff. (And we all have stuff.) One of my favorite phrases to use when I am training a group of managers is this: We can either deal with things, or deal with the consequences of not dealing with things. If you have been mistreated at work, especially by superiors who either exploited or disregarded you, counseling may help you work through the fallout from those experiences. I am a big believer in therapy, and some of my greatest revelations have come from this. Rebuilding your corporate self-image and proceeding confidently and authentically is possible, but women who have been subjugated or harassed must do their own personal healing work concurrently. If you have showed up cowed by previous abuse, or overly aggressive as a shield, true progress will come when you feel secure enough to show up as the woman you are—nothing more, nothing less.

This practice of "being true to yourself," according to Susannah, encompasses everything from the way a woman expresses herself to the way she dresses and accessorizes. Rather than attempting to disappear by choosing bland clothing or using outfits as a weapon to gain attention, women who are confident in themselves in the workplace can find the balance that expresses their personality while remaining appropriate to their specific setting.

"I used to be so uncomfortable doing things I loved because I thought it put a spotlight on my femininity," Susannah said. "I love nail polish and makeup, and it took me until three or four years into my career to be comfortable with those in a professional setting. I didn't want to do anything that made it even more obvious I was a woman. I've learned, as I've gained age and experience. that if something as trivial as nail polish or eye shadow is what keeps me from being successful in someone's eyes, then I never stood a chance!"

Camille has also leaned into expressing her femininity and individuality through her clothing, and as she has mentored other women she has discovered that her self-expression conveys confidence and frees her coworkers to be more authentic as well. "I've had women tell me, 'You coming here has made me feel like I can be more like myself.' When I first joined the company, our CFO dressed so conservatively, almost very masculine, and now the way she dresses is entirely different. I'm a senior leader and I'm going to dress like a woman. And I talk about my children and I talk about my life. I think that at one point, I just kind of said, 'screw it.' I'm a woman and hear me roar, and I don't worry about it."

Find a Mentor. Be a Mentor. Several women talked about the importance of mentors in helping a **Tess** find her voice and show up effectively for her distinct role in the workplace. As Ellen pointed out, the greater number of women who work and lead in a space, the easier those who have been embattled in the past can find it to be genuine and even vulnerable. "Being surrounded by women, it's easier to be your authentic self," she said. "So in my prior roles, where I was the only woman, I would try to be more like the men, you know, more assertive, which was not my authentic self."

Katelyn, who is naturally a strong personality and tends to communicate with a blunt forthrightness, said that her workplace mentor helps her to know when to dial it back and bring a softer touch to a situation.

From her role in human resources, Charlene has frequent opportunities to advocate for women who have truly been harassed or belittled. She said that she has had to confront male managers who touch female employees inappropriately, recalling one instance when an executive responded, "Well, she's like a daughter to me." Charlene told the man that his employee was not his daughter, and she moved the needle at that organization toward fairness and decency while reminding embattled female employees that they don't stand alone.

Another step toward helping **Tess** show up authentically at work is identifying the ways that her femininity, or perhaps even the roles that she plays outside of the office, can enhance her effectiveness with clients or coworkers. In her dental practice, Michelle said that her own process toward finding comfort in her professional skin has been relating to patients on a more personal level. "When I first started practicing I would try to put on a persona to impress people, but now I think my patients get the true me," she said. "I'll sit and chat about my kids or what I'm making for dinner while I'm working. I think it's actually helped me because people can see I'm a person too, and not just a mean dentist out of horror stories. I also like to highlight the amazing qualities of being a female in my role like smaller hands and a gentler touch, or even the fact that as a mom I understand a lot of the struggles parents are going through and can brainstorm solutions with them."

The women who thrive despite a history of incidents that could have turned them into **Tess** are those who seek out wisdom from mentors, believe in their voice, and refuse to frame themselves as victims. Lucy emphasized this point because she has often seen women who are too quick to take offense and turn a minor skirmish into a war, all at the expense of collaboration and effectiveness. "I think women blame 'male culture', but they shouldn't," she said. "They have every ability to succeed at work, but not if they are going to act like victims, gang up against men, or poison the culture by complaining that they don't get their fair share. I think most workplaces value women and if not, they need to find a new place to work. Women have power, women have choices, and saying they don't isn't really true."

For a manager or coworker who wants to help a colleague find her way out of the turmoil **Tess's** past damage can cause, the soundest advice our experts offer is to remind her that each woman brings something unique to an assignment and she will perform her best, and connect with others the most authentically, when she recognizes the part only she can play. "Don't apologize for who you are," said Amy. "Whether it's someone like me who's really strong and has a strong personality and wants to take the reins and control it, or someone who is more quiet. Own who you are, and know that it's okay."

My Road

It is funny to look back now and see how the period of burnout and disengagement at Exxon helped prepare my path for my future work. I know this is why I became so passionate about the concept of employee engagement. I was the poster person for disengagement and burnout leading to a job change. I also look back on the discussion with my boss about my interests, and the fact that career development conversations were fairly one-sided in those days. There was no room for employees to state what they wanted their career direction to be. Now that I work in talent management, I am quite mindful of the role an employee's wishes need to play in career development conversations. I am happy to see that most companies now do a much better job of ensuring that employee input is valued in career management decisions.

Once I left Exxon, I was only in my new role a few weeks when I learned I was pregnant. What a wonderful blessing after trying for so long! But, it was quite a challenge being new to a company and also dealing with major morning sickness! My boss was understanding, and for that I was thankful. I look back now and see exactly why that nine-month period was so important to my career. At the time, I felt I was wandering a bit. Did I want to continue to work full-time after having my child? Was I crazy to have jumped into this new career trying to establish myself in a new company, only to leave for three months of maternity leave? I could not really answer those questions at the time, so I continued to work one day at a time and learn as much as I could. Everything was planned perfectly for my work up until my due date. I completed certifications to teach several training programs and had dates for all my upcoming training sessions set so I would finish all my big assignments a few weeks before the baby was due. All I needed to do was get through one huge training session, a weeklong event I had planned with people flying in from all over the U.S. to attend, and then I could coast a few weeks until the baby arrived.

The day before the meeting began, I made my daily coffee run to Starbucks (yes, I'd developed a caffeine habit during pregnancy) and had quite a surprise when my water broke right then and there. You know what they say about the best-laid plans? Lesson learned—always, always have a contingency plan. Instead of hosting the training, I had my baby boy, Bradley, the next day. He was absolutely perfect! However, because he was premature and my labor was long, he was at risk of having meningitis. Brad had to stay in the ICU with a spinal tap for three days. My poor, perfect little baby boy had a giant IV in his forehead (Fun fact: even though they called it a spinal tap, the preferred location for it was his head). It was scary, but he was okay, and after three long days he was released.

Given how insurance regulations work, I doubt it will surprise you to hear that I was released before my son was. Gone was my dream of leaving the hospital with Brad in my arms, walking through the door of our home together, and living happily ever after. I went home without him and had to scrub in and wear protective gear to visit him. The day I became a mother was the day I learned my plans no longer ruled the day. Being responsible for another human makes their needs supersede yours, and in my opinion, that is how it should be. I have found comfort over the years in seeking silver linings in trials. Although childbirth did not go as planned, the situation wasn't nearly as bad as it could have been.

Once Brad was home, things went well. He was a happy little guy, slept a lot, and didn't cry too much. I went back to work eleven weeks after Brad was born. That was a long leave back in the nineties! I remember being thankful I hadn't had to go back after six weeks like many women did, since my son was not sleeping through the night at that point and I was at my peak of postpartum exhaustion. I decided to go back to work part-time, working from 8 a.m. to noon each day, but it was still so hard to leave my baby, especially the first few days. Brad was at a daycare facility and he was well cared for there. The next Sunday he was getting baptized, and we had a family celebration planned. That Sunday morning I was nursing him and he threw up all down the back of my dress I'd planned to wear to church. And yet we still went through with it! I did decide to take him out of daycare, though, and we found a lovely caregiver who cared for my son in her home. That was a wonderful choice for us.

After a few months back at work, my boss, who was a working mother ten years my senior, told me I could easily work as a contractor if I would like to do so. I thought about it and decided to give it a try. I purchased a computer, and that is how I started my company. I figured I would only work as a contractor for a year or so until I was ready to resume my full-time role. Little did I know this was the beginning of an eighteen-year journey that would take me all over the world! A few months into my contract gig, my boss left. I was sad to see her go, and I heard some rumblings that my employer might also be cutting back on its budget to pay contractors like me.

I was weighing my options when—surprise—I learned I was pregnant with my second child! After struggling to get pregnant the first time around and then delivering Brad prematurely, I was told by my obstetrician to take it easy with this pregnancy. I ended up reducing my workload, and we decided to move. Doing so meant losing my great childcare provider, and midway through my pregnancy, due to these changes, I became a stay-at-home mom. I would not trade that time at home with my son for anything! It allowed us to meet new friends in the neighborhood—both moms and toddlers—and establish a new routine. I was thankful to have my contract gig as well, since once I had this baby I could keep my resumé current even if I only facilitated one learning session a month.

My daughter Bethany was born that fall. I carried her full term, and there were no delivery complications this time. I found the adjustment from having one to two children rough. It didn't help that she cried. A LOT. She wanted to nurse all the time and seemed rather uncomfortable. I was oh-so-thankful Brad was easygoing, because his baby sister was definitely not. When Bethany was about six months old, she had a terrible urinary tract infection that led us to the ER one night. Soon after, we learned she had a condition that made some of her urine back up into her kidneys instead of exiting through her bladder. She had a twenty percent chance of outgrowing it by the age of three and was put on prophylactic antibiotics until that time. Although we will never know if that was why she cried so much, we were thankful to know about her diagnosis, have a plan of action, and see an end to the constant crying.

We slowly got into our groove as a family of four. I occasionally facilitated a training session or two, but for the first few years after Bethany was born, I was mostly a stay-at-home mom. Several home-front challenges necessitated that, especially when we learned our house had toxic mold. Brad and Bethany had both been ill a lot, and I have no doubt the mold contributed to it. Both kids had several sets of ear tubes, and Brad was taking allergy shots. We moved out of our home for eight months while the mold was remediated. Between doctor's appointments, rebuilding and remodeling the home after the mold, and going about our day-to-day activities, there was little time to work. I was thankful for the opportunity to be at home with the kids during that time.

I also dabbled with other jobs. I sold scrapbooking materials, since it was my favorite hobby. I was a substitute teacher at my kids' preschool. I continued to lead training sessions and developed training content. Trying to earn a little money "on the side" left me more frazzled than ever, though, and I sometimes wonder if I chose the harder road. At least if I had been working full-time, we would have had a more predictable schedule and income. But two things led me to decide not to work full-time—first, the tug on my heartstrings of wanting to be there for all my kids' big moments and the feeling that I would never see them if I worked all day every day. The conversations I had previously about not wanting a nanny raising my children ran through my head whenever I thought about returning to full-time work. Second, my husband had a great job and made more money than I did (more on that later).

So, I continued to have one foot in the stay-at-home mom club and the other in juggling part-time gigs. Soon I realized that the scrapbooking business took me away from my family on a lot of evenings and weekends, and the pay at the preschool was a fraction of what my contract training business could bring in. A friend finally suggested I concentrate on growing my training business, and so I did. I did learn a lot from those side gigs though; I firmly believe that we can take away something from every experience we go through. I learned that even though I once thought I wanted to be a schoolteacher, I did not possess nearly enough patience to teach children. This was later confirmed when I taught Sunday School! I also learned one very valuable piece of advice from my scrapbooking community. Someone told me you have to decide if your business is a charity, a hobby, or truly a business. That guided me as I turned my focus to building my consulting firm.

—⁓—

"I have come to the frightening conclusion that **I am the decisive element.** It is my personal approach that **creates the climate.** It is my daily mood that makes the weather. I possess tremendous power to **make life miserable or joyous.** I can be a tool of torture or an instrument of inspiration, I can humiliate or humor, hurt or heal. In all situations, it is my response that decides whether a crisis is escalated or de-escalated, and a person is humanized or de-humanized. If we treat people as they are, we make them worse. If we treat people as they ought to be, **we help them become** what they are capable of becoming."

JOHANN WOLFGANG VON GOETHE

CHAPTER SIX

Caring Enough to Choose to Be Seen

In the wake of the isolation and disillusionment many felt through the COVID-19 pandemic, a new workplace trend called "quiet quitting" became a hot topic in the media. Suddenly employees were opening up about their practice of doing the bare minimum at work, of staying disengaged, and declining opportunities to have a voice or a leadership role in their organization. Motives for "quiet quitting" vary widely, but at the heart of the idea is a woman we call **Invisible Isabella**.

Not every **Invisible Isabella** would characterize herself as a quiet quitter, but **Isabella** does often fade into the background, whether because she doesn't want to make her presence known or because she doesn't believe she has anything to contribute. Her commitment to the mission of the organization and to her teammates is typically rather low, and she is prone to telling people what she believes they want to hear rather than risking a confrontation. Her way of showing up at work can look like simple laziness, but inevitably there is more to **Isabella's** lack of engagement.

Isabella may have formed these tendencies in her childhood, especially if her voice was disregarded when she was growing up or she was led to believe that keeping the peace was more valuable than expressing her opinion. It is also possible that poor leadership from parents or authority figures served to effectively silence her. **Isabella** may feel stuck and powerless. She might be easy to get along with like **Lovable Lila,** but she is more likely to be a pushover in group settings, unwilling or unable to advocate for her position. She is typically conflict-averse and is known as the last person in the office who would make waves. Because "going along to get along" is at the core of her work philosophy, **Isabella** seems to disappear into the woodwork, diminishing her value to the team and the organization.

There is another important reason women may turn into **Isabellas** at work. I have worked often with employee surveys over the years, and I find it fascinating to look at what often happens within the first ninety days of starting a new job. Employees are typically excited and eager on their first day. By the time they get to day ninety, surveys have shown time and again that many new employees become quite disillusioned. This can occur for so many reasons. Perhaps the employee didn't have a smooth onboarding process. Their computer and office supplies weren't ready, or they spent hours with IT trying to get a working email address. Maybe they were not effectively oriented to the new job and were instead thrown into chaos and left to figure it out on their own without proper resources. Those external factors certainly have an impact.

Consider also the impact of employee gossip, general morale, and a weak leader supervising the new employee. It saddens me to see how often and how quickly employees can disengage. All too often, managers lament these perceived lazy employees and scratch their heads trying to figure out how to get more productivity from them. Yet the managers lack the self-awareness to consider that they indeed may be the root of the problem! Even seasoned leaders often fail to recognize that even an employee with extensive experience may still have a steep learning curve to acclimate to a specific company culture.

When managers dismiss ideas, fail to check in and guide new employees while they learn the job, or demonstrate any number of other weak leadership behaviors, they may unintentionally be creating the very **Isabellas** that vex them later on. This may even lead to companies hiring a revolving door of new soon-to-be **Isabellas** reporting to the same leaders. Before they know it, the ineffective leader has cycled through several employees and has succumbed to a vicious cycle. When that becomes the norm, it is time for the company to reevaluate whether that leader should truly be managing people. I believe this is a major reason that over time so many women become progressively less engaged and more invisible.

Coverage of the "quiet quitting" phenomenon focused on younger employees, suggesting a generational difference in attitudes toward commitment and loyalty. It would be far too simplistic to suggest that younger people don't work as hard; laziness and diligence are characteristics of every age group. But just as companies don't tend to be as loyal to their employees as they were several decades ago, those entering the workforce today seem to be more effective in keeping various sectors of their lives distinct. They want to work for a paycheck, but many are unwilling to expend their emotional energy to develop loyalty for a job or company that doesn't value them or extend loyalty to them in return.

An August 2022 survey conducted by resumebuilder.com surveyed 1,000 workers representing a range of ages. When asking the respondents about their level of effort at the office, the researchers found that thirty percent of those surveyed between the ages of 25 and 34 reported doing the "bare minimum," whereas only eight percent of those over 54 said the same. "The trend appears to be shaped by generational changes, with Gen Z and millennial workers increasingly questioning the hustle culture embedded within corporate America against the backdrop of the pandemic," said a CBSnews.com article about "quiet quitting."

These younger **Invisible Isabellas** may be determined to simply "punch a clock" without investing much of themselves into their jobs. Giving the bare minimum robs them of satisfaction that comes from using their talents fully to complete their tasks with excellence. There is always a risk of swinging too far the other way toward workaholism, but

Isabellas who learn to lean into their job can find a new level of meaning and gratification. Their results—and their relationships with coworkers—will improve, and they might find that work becomes less an obligation and more a pleasure.

In the same way, young employees are often seeking fulfillment and meaning in their jobs, and those ideals make them critical of work that doesn't seem, on its face, to have significance. These individuals dismiss the day-to-day responsibilities of a job as simply a grind, or just a path to a paycheck, but investing themselves in those tasks might be the very path to finding deeper meaning. The intangibles of a workplace—factors like diligence, community, strong leadership, and excellence—can show a would-be **Isabella** that an "everyday" job has more potential to shape her and others than she once thought. Additionally, when I look back on some of these seemingly mundane roles, I quickly realize how much I learned from them. It is unrealistic to expect to walk into a job and do only very meaningful things. Ultimately, the questions to consider are whether the meaningful parts of your role outweigh the mundane ones, and whether you are learning and growing in the role. Ask yourself whether this is truly a dead end, or a means to move on to something bigger and more fulfilling in time.

I remember the first **Invisible Isabella** I worked with—let's call her Leigh. She had been in the job longer than most and had a different career path than the rest of us. While most of us were just passing through the job en route to bigger and better things, she was a professional in her territory management role and was the one who would teach us the ropes. It was easy to understand why she was cynical. She knew the job and was good at it. She had to watch a never-ending parade of new employees, many of whom had just graduated a month or so earlier, walk in to learn the job and then move on to bigger, better roles while she remained in the same one. Looking back, I doubt the company did anything to compensate her for training us; they probably just expected her to do it.

I found it a challenge—the kind of challenge I wanted to conquer—to build a relationship with Leigh. She was very, very different than me. Leigh came through the ranks working at a gas station, moving up to manage one, and eventually rising to be a territory manager. She did not go to college, and that became a factor in how she was treated by the company. I find it fascinating to look back on that now. At the time, it seemed normal to me that there were "haves" and "have-nots" in the workplace.

Driven by my need for acceptance, I worked hard to try to win Leigh over. Over time, I found things we had in common—from our love of similar foods to our sense of humor—and we worked together on a few projects. I'd like to think perhaps I helped her soften her abruptness, but the truth is, she probably changed me more than I changed her. I am so glad I made an effort to get to know Leigh, because I have come across so many more **Invisible Isabellas** since this first encounter. They were all so different than me. I'm an open book, from what I say, to how I show what I am thinking.

Leigh, on the other hand, had a great poker face. She would take it all in and avoid reacting at all. She would occasionally make sarcastic comments so we would all know she was none too pleased, and we were all pretty intimidated by her. I have wondered if her negativity might have been hiding some deep-seated fears about venturing into the unknown, or if she secretly relished the silent power she wielded in her roles. Because we didn't really know how to relate to Leigh, people tended to remain curiously distanced from her. This gave Leigh power in the office dynamic, which I think she enjoyed.

Some of the women we surveyed about their workplace experiences confirmed that they have at some point downplayed their own potential and behaved as **Invisible Isabellas**. Carmen said that she has noticed that she as well as other women in her workplace tend to downplay their skills. This tendency is especially apparent when someone praises a woman for her performance at work. Rather than accept the compliment, too many women deflect it, afraid of drawing attention to themselves or seeming proud. Amy Morin, the author of *13 Things Mentally Strong People Don't Do*, cited research studies showing that while men often tend to overplay their strong points, women are prone to minimizing their achievements. "It's important for women to give themselves credit when it's due," Morin wrote in an article for Inc.com. "Rather than shrink themselves to help other people feel comfortable or downplay their efforts, it's important for women to be able to own their achievements."

In her role as a business coach, Taylor said she has seen too many women diminish their strengths and subsequently rob themselves of advancement opportunities. She has even had conversations with CEOs who tell her that they think a certain woman in the organization has the capability and talent to be the next CEO. But when Taylor spends time coaching that high-potential employee, she finds that the employee is more comfortable fading into the background. "When I speak with her, the employee says, 'I know that the request is for me to work on my confidence, but I just feel so intimidated around those with authority,'" Taylor said. "And I think, oh, here she is sitting with a golden opportunity to be the next CEO. And what's standing in her way is her feeling that she is not worthy of that."

TRAPS: PITFALLS TO AVOID

As we have already mentioned, the drawbacks of showing up as an **Isabella** include an incapacity to develop strong relationships in the workplace and a limiting effect on potential advancement, but those aren't the only traps that come into play if you become invisible. As Taylor discovered with her coaching clients, **Isabellas** have a disturbing tendency to underestimate themselves. Karla, a college professor in a male-dominated area of study, said that she has appointed herself as a cheerleader for women who undersell their potential to thrive in a position or excel at a task.

"Overall, I think the biggest mistake other women make is not trusting themselves and their abilities," Karla said. "I see women sell themselves short all the time. Men will apply for any job even if they know they aren't qualified, while women won't even apply for jobs they are overqualified for. Observing this has impacted me. I've realized few people tell others when they notice something they are gifted at. I've become an encourager and tend to push others when I see their gifts at work."

Chloe gets frustrated with herself when she settles for less than she deserves in the workplace because, as she said, "You're the only person that can advocate for yourself." Chloe adds, "I'm not a good negotiator in terms of salary and things in my contract because I just kind of take what I'm offered and run with it. And I wish that I was stronger in that area. I feel like if I ask for things that I'll be looked down on. I don't know what it is in our DNA that makes us feel like we can't advocate for ourselves or ask for what we want."

Anya, who like Karla works in a university setting, had to go to bat for herself and fellow women at the college because for years women had been settling for smaller salaries that were not commensurate with their positions or workloads. Those historical inequalities, caused by women who believed they were powerless to fight the situation, have created a more treacherous road for the women in today's organizations who know better. "The impact on me personally was seeing smaller salaries that the male treasurer at my university felt should be okay and having to go to bat for many of my female staff members, as well as myself, to get increases," Anya said.

When women retreat into their **Isabella** stance instead of speaking up for themselves or advocating for their perspective, they miss the chance to contribute to the organization in a meaningful way, and the company is less effective because of their silence. In some cases, **Isabellas** are complicit in their workplace boundaries being disregarded, because they allow themselves to be overworked or taken advantage of. Chloe recounted the story of a coworker who insisted that she had to leave the office at 3 p.m. every day because of obligations to her children; Chloe never said anything about it, but as her coworker maintained a work-life balance, Chloe found that she herself was working longer hours than she should have been. "She actually won in that situation," she said of her coworker.

Another limiting factor of an **Isabella**, as Lucy has observed in her workplace, is the fear of learning new skills and pursuing enriching opportunities. A certain degree of risk-taking is required for anyone who wants to make a difference and reach new heights in their job. But **Isabella's** lack of confidence, her failure to see herself as someone who could solve intricate problems or bring people together in a meaningful way, often keeps her stuck in place. "A mistake I see women make is being afraid and acting like a victim, not being flexible and willing to step up to learn and apply new skills," she said.

The more **Isabella** separates herself from the vision and purpose of her workplace, especially when she fails to pursue true connections with coworkers, the more prone she is to feel lonely and unfulfilled. And in some cases that frustrated state can lead to an unhealthy relationship with emotions, as **Isabella** either stuffs her feelings and looks more disengaged or eventually erupts, when she has suppressed herself for so long that a situation brings all the emotions out at once. Early in her career Camille witnessed several women who were overly emotional. She knew that wasn't appropriate in the workplace, she said, but she has learned that she cannot turn all emotions off in her work interactions.

Those who seem stoic or detached all of the time, like **Isabella**, give the impression that they don't care about their job or the organization. Camille strives to bring appropriate emotion to a situation and hopes to model that to younger women who might feel sad or frustrated at work but don't know how to cope with those feelings. "I've seen women that become very emotional and fall apart over everything because they have no one to go to," she said. "If they really don't have someone that takes them under their wing on purpose, then they're kind of lost."

Ashley had an opportunity to counsel a close friend's daughter who nearly let her emotions run ahead of her to an unwise decision. The young woman called her mother sobbing after her first day of work because her boss had criticized her for making a mistake. She was ready to quit after the first day, and Ashley was able to inject some perspective into the situation. "She felt like it was the end of the world instead of just, well, 'That's life,'" she said. "When you get out of college into the real world, you have to accept that bosses come in all flavors, and your ability to do good work is going to change over time based on your experience."

Isabella certainly can take some responsibility for helping herself rather than fading into the background, but the difficulties associated with invisible employees can often also be laid at the feet of the organizations that hire them but fail to give them a voice. Companies that hire just to occupy a vacant cog in the machine, rather than creating a pipeline for talent that can move up and use their gifts in increasingly valuable ways, reinforce **Isabella's** perception that it's safer to do her job as discreetly as possible. And even when leadership does have a plan in place to develop and advance young employees, they often disregard older employees who have served loyally for a long time, forgetting that they also need to be given a path for growth.

In the cbsnews.com article about "quiet quitting," Ed Zitron, the CEO of the public relations firm EZPR, gives an unflinching view of employees who camp out in bare-minimum territory, pointing out that they often do so because they don't see a reason to exert extra effort for bosses who give scant energy to help them succeed. "It's becoming alarmingly obvious to most workers that there is absolutely no meritocracy—working hard does not mean you'll go far, and going above and beyond rarely, if ever, nets anything other than free work for an uncaring boss," Zitron wrote.

In addition to lackluster talent development, companies allow employees to disengage when they fail to communicate vision to their workforce. A key **Isabella** symptom is a lack of attention to the big picture, but if no one has painted that picture for her, she can hardly be expected to find her place in it. An organization that values its people more highly than its results is largely incompatible with **Isabella** types, because employees there will be drawn in by the power of meaningful work carried out by people who genuinely care about what they are doing.

TECHNIQUES: HOW TO SHOW UP EFFECTIVELY

Explore where you are in your career, where you want to go, and your expectations. If you have been showing up as an **Isabella** and losing your voice along the way, there is a path back to relevance and fulfillment. It starts with conducting a personal inventory of your skills, your values, your goals, and your expectations for your career. Too many **Isabellas** have failed to take account of what they do well, what gratifies them the most, and what success looks like for them. An honest exploration of those variables can then lead to an assessment of your professional expectations. Unmet, misunderstood, or unnamed expectations can all lead to frustration in the workplace, sending **Isabella** further underground. Talking openly about an expectation with a manager, even if that expectation is not able to be met, leads to productive dialogue and eases the tension that comes from staying quiet about what we hope can happen.

When Morgan conducted her own investigation of the factors that had made her feel stuck and inadequate at work, she discovered that she had fallen prey to the comparison trap, diminishing herself when measured against those around her. "The biggest challenge I have faced is the context I created that I was 'less than' because I was growing into my leadership role from an auxiliary role," she said. "My own thought process of how I perceived others saw me was self-limiting. When I began to look at myself differently and recognize that I was my greatest limiting factor, I was able to finally address my own self-doubts and create a new context of who I am."

Evaluate whether you need to make a change. As you peel back the curtain to assess your current situation and the non-negotiables of your work life, you will likely be forced to wrestle with the prospect that another opportunity might be a better fit for you. A clear-eyed survey is important first, because without it an employee is always tempted to think that the grass is greener elsewhere. Only after careful consideration, and a realization that your goals and values are out of alignment with your current organization, is the time ripe to consider a change. Like me and many of our other respondents, Chloe reached a professional fork in the road and knew she needed to start over with a new company. On the other side of her move she knows it was the right step for her, she said, but there were moments when she was tempted to stay with the status quo.

"Thankfully I had about two years of experience, which made it a little bit easier to find something, but not having that comfort of being rooted in an area and having a network of people to help you get your foot in the door was tough," she said. "It worked out great and I became stronger for it, but it was tough to make the decision to pick up and leave."

Some **Isabellas**, restrained by that fear of change, stay in an incompatible situation for far too long, telling themselves that they are parking themselves in an unhealthy job until something better comes along. They know they are in the wrong place so they exert minimum effort, convincing themselves they are being held hostage when the prison is of their own making. These Isabellas are in desperate need of a thorough career inventory and an insightful coach to provide a professional jump start. Don't give up on the prospect of a truly fulfilling job; those positions are out there, and it is often those with a previous track record of disappearing,

Isabella-style, who are able to find and embrace the right opportunity when it does come along. It just requires healthy doses of courage and self-awareness.

Consider new, more productive approaches to handling differences. As each **Isabella** finds her voice, she is bound to also discover a new, healthier perspective on conflict. Whether she was raised to be a quiet peacemaker and she fears making waves or she had a bad experience with a past confrontation, **Isabella** will only thrive when she comes to believe that airing differences is the best path to progress. Amber has noticed that women have a harder time than men managing productive conflict, she said, but she believes it is a skill we should work to perfect. "A lot of women don't know how to manage conflict, to come forward and have constructive conversations," she said. "One statement that I use all the time, that I never hear from other women ever is, 'Hey, I'm concerned that it seems like there's some tension. How can we clear the air?'"

As they become more at ease with differences of opinion, women who tend to be people pleasers start to settle into a revolutionary idea: Not everyone in the workplace is going to agree with you or even like you. Early in her career Laura found that her "sweet personality" made her seem less capable than she really was, and she resolved to offer a stronger side of herself. "I had to toughen up and get some grit," she said.

Maya expresses eloquently what she wants young women in the workplace, those who might suppress their gifts and fade into the background, to know: "Be true to yourself. You are never going to please everyone and that is okay. Someone else's happiness is not your responsibility. We are our own worst critics, and believing you belong at the table is half the battle. Trust yourself and your intuition. It's a gift, and especially as women, we tend to suppress it. Most of the time, people only see what is visible now and make assumptions. What they don't see is all of the hard work, time, energy, failures, and sacrifices that it took to get to this place. That's okay; you don't have anything to prove to anyone but yourself."

Be open to a range of people and ideas. In my first job, where I worked with Leigh, there were a lot of people I supervised who were from quite different walks of life than me. Generally, the people working in the gas stations I managed didn't go to college; some did not finish high school, and many were new to the United States. Many of them made minimum wage or slightly higher, and they usually worked more than one job to make ends meet. I learned through this experience that we all have more in common than we might first realize. When we can seek to find common ground, and treat others with respect, life is richer and work is better. Attributes like integrity, intelligence, and communication skills transcend socio-economic and cultural differences.

If I had walked into that first job with an attitude that I was better than the people I managed, what a mistake that would have been. I have always tried to approach people who are different than me as humans, seeing them and respecting them for who they are. It's not always easy to do this, as I have had to fight some of the stereotypical reactions running through my subconscious mind when I encounter some new situations outside my comfort zone. Figuring out how to relate to those who are different has helped me more than I can express over the past thirty-plus years. I believe it's what led me to be effective at facilitating manager training with front-line supervisors.

The funny thing is that eventually I realized I preferred to work with people who had less formal education versus more. The people who thought they were the smartest in the room rarely thought they had anything to learn. (And usually they had far more to learn, especially about the art of interacting with different people!) Years later I took the StrengthsFinder® from Gallup, and it finally made sense why I took this approach with people. My top strength was Individualization, which is explained as follows: "People who are especially talented in the individualization theme are intrigued with the unique qualities of each person. They have a gift for figuring out how people who are different can work together productively." Maybe it was Leigh, my first **Invisible Isabella,** who helped me become the leader I am. Even if it was driven by some kind of sick need within me to win her over, I can definitely say I am better for it. This was a difference-maker in my career.

I've gotten to the point that I can almost bet that things are truly about halfway between my optimistic assessment and **Invisible Isabella's** pessimistic one. What makes me sad about **Isabella** is that I wonder what has made her so cynical, and whether she is missing out on the joy that can accompany a new idea, a fresh perspective, or a positive outlook. When I have managed an **Isabella** on my team, I would try to put her in a position to share her perspectives as a subject matter expert and provide incentives that might motivate her to give more discretionary effort. It didn't always change her attitude, but it offered her an opportunity to grow in her role.

To those **Invisible Isabellas** out there reading this, does presenting this way at work decrease your stress level, or might it instead be making life more difficult for you? I suspect in many cases it might be the latter. If that is true for you, I suggest you find a way to let go of grudges, and especially examine whether the people around you now are the ones who wronged you, or whether you have carried these burdens around for so long that they have outlived the relationships that spawned them.

—⁂—

My Road

Once I hit my stride with both kids, I focused on consulting instead of going back into the corporate world full-time. I never thought I would remain a consultant for eighteen years; I did not plan that far ahead. I used to describe myself as an "accidental entrepreneur," and whenever anyone asked me what I did for a living, I would say my job was to make my kids think I worked as little as possible. In retrospect, having the ability to be home with my kids, make it to their school programs, get dinner on the table, and manage my own company was the most incredibly difficult—no, scratch that, it was impossible—balancing act I had ever attempted.

During these years, I lived by the calendar. The kids' birthdays were always blocked off, and there were many times I missed conferences and revenue opportunities to avoid ever missing their birthdays. After that, priorities on the calendar each year were the first and last days of school and key holidays. I did my best to always honor those dates. I also blocked out time for every school program I could, and when the kids got older, I blocked out their sporting events. Although I couldn't make it to every single game, I made it to most of them. Also, a special shout-out to all the moms who were my carpool buddies for years! You know who you are, and you made it possible for me to work when I needed to and know that my kids were in great hands! A few of these amazing moms even took photos at all the events, and that was such a gift. I felt like I got the highlights from them even if I had to miss something. I always tried to return the favor. Lesson learned—surround yourself with like-minded people and cultivate those friendships. They will probably be some of your best friends long after your kids have grown and flown.

There was something very special about watching the same kids grow up from babyhood through college and on to their own marriages and kids. It was as if we moms grew up together too! In some cases, our children were best buddies. In others, they really didn't hang out together much. In a few cases, we moms had to have a conversation about keeping our friendships separate from our kids' friendships, which helped a lot. The funny thing is that looking back now, in a few cases the kids who didn't really hang out growing up ended up being close later after high school. Maybe they had classes together, went to the same college, or had mutual friends. It is nice to see how these friendships evolved over time on their own—without our "help" or interference!

One lesson learned—one of the worst things you can do for your kids and yourself is to try to project your own issues, desires, or wishes on your children. Heaven help the child whose parents are helicopter parents! If we think women in the workplace are competitive, they've got nothing on the uber-competitive type-A helicopter moms I encountered! And for what? All the kids will end up on the path they need to be on, and rarely do their parents' excessive interventions help them. It just makes life much more difficult for teachers, coaches, and other adults trying to pour into these kids.

I learned the hard way that I needed to pray that I would not let the trials of my children's days ruin mine. For the first few years of elementary school, when the kids came home and told me another kid had been mean to them, I reacted too much. I was sad for them, which was probably appropriate as a parent, but I got so frustrated by the mean kids. I am thankful my kids weren't mean, but kids will be kids and I couldn't let myself get so frustrated. Once I was able to talk with them and give some practical advice like telling them to find someone else to play with on the playground, our discussions became more productive. And sometimes just remembering that "this too shall pass" was all that was needed.

When my kids were little, I created a cocoon of sorts, attempting to guard against them hearing bad language, modeling good behavior even though that was sometimes tough to do, and teaching them right from wrong. There comes a point, though, when kids begin to pick up on things. I remember the time my son's preschool teacher told me my son had uttered two curse words that day. I was so embarrassed when the teacher told me, and she laughed and said, "Well, the good news is that he knew how to use them in proper context." Oh, how I appreciated the grace that teacher showed me that day.

My son came home from school in first grade and told me someone on the bus said the f-word. I said, "Oh, they said the f-word, huh?" I was simply reflecting back what I thought I'd heard, because I couldn't think of anything better to say. He then said, "Yes, mom," he said emphatically. "He said fart!" I nearly doubled over with laughter and relief. Oh, that they would stay that innocent forever! But by the time he was ten or eleven, my son began to watch shows like *The Office* and I decided it was okay. We watched these shows together and used some of the more mature subjects as an opportunity to talk about learning moments. I appreciate that my kids understand sarcasm and have a great sense of humor. I like to think that allowing them the opportunity to watch TV and experience typical teenage things helped more than it hurt. Some of the kids whose parents kept them in cocoons became the wildest kids by the time they could drive. It was sad to see, and in many cases the kids came around and their rebellion was just a phase.

In the end, what does all this worry do for us parents? Striving to be perfect, be above it all, and avoid trouble is a recipe for frustration and heartache in many cases. I tried that, and it didn't last too long or end too well. Being real and being vulnerable—admitting I was imperfect and that I didn't have all the answers—seemed to work far better for me.

One perk of having my own business was that we got to enjoy some great family trips combined with my work engagements. The kids will tell me they loved these trips and are thankful they had the chance to travel so much. However, it wasn't always realistic for them to join me, so even though I was fulfilling a personal goal to travel internationally for work, if my family wasn't with me I would complete the trip as quickly as possible. Often I didn't see many of the sights in some beautiful countries. One of the things I jokingly tell my friends is that conference rooms look the same all over the world. Lesson learned—take advantage of the opportunity to travel. Try to build in some time to sightsee. You never know if you will have a chance to get back there.

—◊—

"No one can make you feel inferior without your consent."

ELEANOR ROOSEVELT

CHAPTER SEVEN

Moving Beyond the "Like" Button

When a manager describes an employee, or an athlete, as the "ultimate team player," it is seen as the highest praise. But some women, in the interest of keeping the peace and achieving harmonious collaboration with everyone around them, place their ability to work with others above everything else, and they lose their voice along the way. Meet **Lovable Lila.**

If **Cool Camryn** is insulated from the community and overly protective of her emotions, **Lovable Lila** is her flip side. Everybody in a workplace loves **Lila** and enjoys having her on their team. She prefers working collaboratively to going it alone, she knows everyone's name, and above all she wants to be liked by her coworkers and managers. Those around her are quick to ask her for help, which she willingly gives.

Lovable Lila is motivated by the desire to function as a valuable member of the community. She is often a people pleaser in her personal as well as her professional life, and she has either avoided conflict at all costs in her past or been so burned by a previous disagreement that she has vowed to keep the peace at all costs. Beneath the likable exterior lies a fear of being the odd one out or adopting a position that will make others uncomfortable.

At first blush **Lila** seems like an asset to an organization, and her relational skills do contribute to a congenial environment. But **Lila** is selling herself and others short when she adheres so closely to a peacemaker persona that she misses opportunities to be an advocate and an influencer.

When she prioritizes the status quo out of a fear of rocking the boat, **Lila,** and sometimes even her team, misses the opportunity to grow. **Lila's** relational equity has probably earned her the collateral to successfully represent the interest of others to her superiors, but she is hesitant to enter into those conversations. She is unable to manage up because her focus is fixed on her team. This myopic way of showing up impairs **Lila,** robbing her of vision for the big picture of the organization and her power to enrich both the company and the coworkers she cares about.

Not only does **Lila** struggle to wield true influence in the workplace, she can also fall victim to porous boundaries that lead to unhealthy work situations. Jan said that she is disheartened when she sees women who allow themselves to be taken advantage of professionally by clients. Driven by a desire to please clients and to be seen as helpful and kind, these **Lilas** go too high above and too far beyond, leading clients to expect more than they should and creating unrealistic frameworks for others who do the same job.

Sally places a high value on getting along well with others at work, but she has internalized that tendency to an extreme because of misguided feedback from male coworkers. These men, positioning themselves as "coaches" for Sally, have told her that she can intimidate others, even labeling her an "alpha female." Instead of encouraging her to use her gifts and her influence, these so-called advisors extinguish any efforts to assert her leadership. "I am highly introspective, so I will look to see where I am accountable first and try to make adjustments to help others to be more comfortable," she said. "This can result in my realizing that I am acting less my authentic self and more a role to be 'pleasing to others.'"

Lovable Lila might be tempted to find a comfortable place in an organization and camp out there, Ashley said. **Lila** could be blocked by feedback like Sally received, either verbal or nonverbal, which suggests that women shouldn't put themselves forward to seek advancement or pursue solutions to problems they see. As Ashley says, "They're afraid of not being the Girl Scout who does everything right and delivers all the cookies on time." They find a level where they know their job expectations and where they are confident they can succeed, and the longer they stay there the more they fear stepping out. "I see women not stepping up to the plate, not living in the gap where you really have to stretch to achieve the next level," she said. "I've seen that over and over and over, where I've managed people who I've pushed to do more impactful projects, work with more senior executives, and they're afraid of it."

Criticisms of professional women, that they are overbearing or too dominant, produce environments that encourage **Lovable Lila** to stay in her lane and get along with everybody. But even if those dynamics can be unhealthy for both the women and their companies, the emphasis on relationships favored by **Lilas** can be a strong example to more self-centered employees who disregard the importance of community. As Tasha has observed, "I believe women tend to form more of a relationship-building style whereas men tend to control, dominate, or lead a conversation. I've noticed that working with mostly women, all ideas are respected and encouraged. There is less of an ego-driven environment and more of team building."

When a **Lovable Lila** is motivated by a drive to bring out the best in herself and her organization, and those goals can be achieved by working in collaborative harmony, her relational gifts will motivate and produce results. But that vision of a more fully developed **Lila** can only be reached when people-pleasing is removed from the equation. Charlene might have classified herself as a **Lila** early in her career, because she was so bent on being friends with everyone in her workplace that she struggled to see that her road to peak effectiveness would include plenty of rough spots. "I used to think everybody needed to like me, but then I realized that was never gonna happen," she said. "The bottom line is, you can't have everyone like you, but they need to respect you. If you're somewhere where people don't really respect you, you're not going to get where you need to go."

TRAPS: PITFALLS TO AVOID

We have already mentioned that **Lovable Lila**, despite being a sought-after team member, is liable to weaken her own voice and her ability to advocate because of her commitment to keeping the peace no matter what. But showing up as a **Lila** puts women at risk of falling into other traps that diminish her effectiveness at work and, more crucially, damage her belief in herself to manage others and push for personal and organizational growth. Even if you place a high value on relationships, participating in community in the workplace doesn't look the same as community in your personal life. What are the pitfalls of failing to observe boundaries or incorrectly prioritizing camaraderie?

Miriam cautions that women in the workplace tend to get so invested in the possibility of friendships that they confide too much. A fine line exists between making authentic connections with coworkers and spilling everything about yourself in a professional setting. "Women have the tendency to not know when to keep things to themselves," she said. "They tend to trust everyone, feeling as if they can confide in another female worker, but then it can backfire on them. I have learned what confidentiality truly means." This propensity for oversharing can bring serious fallout, especially if a **Lila** shares inappropriately about her personal life or confides in a coworker who might use information against her. It's enough to turn a **Lila** into a **Cool Camryn**, but the goal is to strike a prudent balance between relational openness and guardedness.

Oversharing at work is often motivated by a fundamental need to belong, and wise managers will promote company and team loyalty to remind their people that they do, in fact, have a valued community at work. But this concept can be stretched too far, as in the case of confiding too much, and it can also result in a clannishness that pits one team against another and inhibits a **Lila** who wants to lead outside the boundaries of her team. A **Lovable Lila** can expend all of her energy strengthening team ties and then look up and realize that her team is a silo—disconnected from the broader vision of the organization and hindered in cooperating with those on other teams.

Some of the specific trials that trip up **Lilas** are a direct result of the "boys club" within their organizations. She tries to be a good teammate and to relate well to coworkers, but in some settings the men put up walls of their own and make it difficult for women to show up as their true selves. Morgan works in a male-dominated industry, and even though she has seen some progress in the way she is treated, she still faces a disconnect between the "old guard" way of doing business and a more collaborative, relational way that is usually inspired by the women in the room. Tasha has found more freedom in a workplace of mostly women, in a space not driven by egos, but women working in a predominantly male space, like Morgan, can be targets of criticism that is less about their performances and more about gender differences.

"While barriers have been lifted significantly and I have been able to earn respect through my work ethic and how I treat people, the good ole boys club still lives in small pockets throughout the industry," Morgan said. "I am so sick of men (it is never women) who tell me I am 'too nice.' No, I am professional and treat people the way I would expect to be treated myself. This is the lingering patriarchy that continues, that is disguised as an acceptable form of feedback from the men I work with to this day. It's diminishing and diminutive and I am quick to correct anyone who tries to marginalize me with this descriptor."

Alice has faced another type of obstacle in her effort to forge connections with male coworkers—the predominance of social activities in business settings that are skewed toward men. She has gone on too many business trips whose schedules are peppered with hunting or golf outings, experiences that exclude her. While her coworkers are spending the afternoon on the golf course, Alice will schedule a spa day for herself, she said, but even as she does so, she knows she is missing out on opportunities to strengthen ties with coworkers and possibly even clients. For women who lean toward the best qualities of a **Lila,** who value strong teams and want to thrive as a part of them, this type of exclusion is particularly troublesome.

Since **Lila** sees so much value in collaboration, she can also get caught in an environment where siloed work is the expectation, and she struggles to thrive where her relational skills aren't valued. Such was the case for Susan, who decided to leave a job after a manager characterized her efforts to work effectively with others as a distraction. "He told me, 'You know, you just can't stay in your lane. You're getting a lot of things done, but you're also getting distracted by trying to collaborate and connect the dots. And we just need you to focus,'" Susan said. "So I went home, and over the weekend I went to my neighbor's pool, and I floated in the pool for a little bit, and I said, 'Well, I'm obviously in the wrong place. If you don't value the fact that I'm trying to be collaborative, and I'm trying to build something, we're just creating a lot of silos. And I don't think that's right.'"

In some cases skewing towards **Lovable Lila** can lead to discouragement or even, as in Susan's case, facilitate the end of a woman's time in a company. Other times **Lila** has seasons of contentment in her position because of her many friendships, but she eventually realizes she is stuck because fear of making waves has inhibited her from confronting problems or advocating for positive change. Holly has found, over the course of her career in human services and education, that the more confrontational parts of managing people did not come easily, and she has struggled to develop the confidence to enter into hard discussions when it becomes necessary. On one occasion she opted to leave a job because she was so often called on to carry out burdensome tasks that forced her to deliver difficult news to another person.

TECHNIQUES:
HOW TO SHOW UP EFFECTIVELY

Many of the qualities that define **Lovable Lilas** are both admirable and beneficial for thriving in the workplace, but the issues arise when a **Lila** values her effectiveness at relationships above anything else and loses the through line of growth and innovation. Women who are stuck in **Lila** mode don't need to reinvent themselves as much as recognize how to use their collaborative superpowers for the greater good:

Seek to accumulate "relationship collateral." **Lila** understands intuitively how to form, grow, and sustain healthy relationships within an organization; interacting in a meaningful way with others is the most significant part of her work experience. But if she collects all of that relationship collateral and never spends it in the interest of the company's goals, she is a little bit like Scrooge McDuck, perched atop his mountain of gold coins. If keeping the peace and being a friend to everyone is your chief goal, you will stockpile the relationship collateral that could have allowed you to redirect a teammate whose actions are working against the team's goals. That collateral could also allow you to advocate for employees under you who don't have as much favor with the company's leadership. In short, a **Lila** can work for healthy change when she recognizes how much relational wealth she has and starts to give it away to worthy causes.

Everyone wants to know that they are trusted by their coworkers, but ultimately being trusted isn't enough. You have to take that trustworthiness, which is a form of relationship collateral, and expend it by advocating for others. By actively demonstrating, through actions for the good of the team and the company, that you deserve trust, you can help transform the culture of an organization and make it more effective besides. A happy team is never the ultimate goal, because a team populated by **Lovable Lilas** might feel great about their relationships but still be blissfully ignorant about their lack of productivity and the organization's health. As Curt Coffman writes, "Happy cows don't provide better milk."

Show leadership courage. A **Lila** who wants to be a more effective leader can move her team from an overemphasis on harmony to an environment that supports healthy and productive conflict, characterized by respectfully addressing differences in the interest of becoming better. Great teams debate ideas while still respecting the people on either side of those debates. They honor individualism but place a high premium on productivity as a team, which is impossible if everyone is stuck on the value of getting along all the time and the **Lilas** with the most relational collateral refuse to make waves. **Lila** might have more influence, and thus more potential to make a difference, than anyone else on her team, but she needs to have the courage to spend her collateral and tap into that influence.

Rena works with mostly men, and she said it has taken her time to become comfortable advocating for herself or others. Early in her career she was too fixated on being a peacemaker, she said, but she found she was in danger of losing herself. "Learning how to navigate situations where I'm treated differently because of my gender was a big challenge to overcome," she said. "The first few times I was in one of these situations, I didn't know how to react and froze. Unfortunately, I have had plenty of opportunities to work on how I react. I've learned that sometimes standing up for yourself is more important than being perceived as easygoing. You can be a good, kind person while also standing up for what you believe in."

As a lifelong people pleaser, Camille also had to discover that doing things for others all the time is not always the best path to a productive, fulfilled team. She loves to take care of others, she said, but the quest to stay in every person's good graces all the time was a dead end. "I just had to recognize that you can't make everybody happy," she said. "Sometimes you have to make hard calls and you just have to take the consequences of those." Likewise, Anita would hardly recognize herself from her earliest years in the workplace, because she was so uncomfortable with negative feedback. Whereas she used to go to great lengths to do everything perfectly so that no one would criticize her, today she knows that feedback, especially the tough kind, is a gift and that it doesn't reflect who she is as a person or as an employee. She has learned to incorporate those critiques, and she has seen that process make her more effective in her job.

Play to your strengths. From her position as a plant manager in a predominantly male industry, Morgan has been able to leverage her best relational qualities into her leadership role, while resisting the urge to mimic the male managers in her company. "I had a conversation recently with one of my male colleagues who told me that I needed to be tougher and more authoritative if I wanted to be a successful plant manager," she said. "I explained to him that I didn't need to lead my team the way he leads his, and that I will continue to be true to my own style of leadership. I also shared that he hadn't seen that side of me, but that it does exist. I just use it judiciously when required."

Generally speaking, women have a greater facility with forging strong relationships in the workplace, with responding to difficult situations thoughtfully and communicating with tact, sensitivity, and authenticity. An over-reliance on relationships can lead a **Lila** to become stuck, to be sure, but if she owns her strengths as a team builder while also recognizing the skills she needs to lead and interact more honestly, she will unlock a new level of influence. That trajectory of growth can lead a recovering **Lila** to embrace unexpected challenges, like Ursula did when a young male dentist joined her practice.

When the new dentist first started working with Ursula, he referred to her as his mentor, which initially took her aback, she said. She didn't see herself as a mentor, particularly for a man in the same position as her, but he valued her example and wanted to learn from her, so she learned to lean into that role. "I had really kind of devalued myself," she said. "I realized, 'okay, I really have a lot to give.' What I saw was that he did not initially realize the importance of relationships with the staff." Ursula was already an influencer, but that mentoring relationship gave her a greater understanding of her ability to create a healthier environment for patients and staff alike in her workplace.

Consider women like Ursula an upgraded, optimized version of **Lovable Lila**: A woman who cares about the people in her organization and continues to maintain meaningful relationships, but marries those skills with boldness and vision as an advocate and a leader.

—⁂—

My Road

When I was so stressed out in my early career, I always dreamed of the day I would have a "stable" job—where I would work a predictable schedule of the same hours each day. Along the way, after I left Exxon and moved into various other jobs, I realized my jobs all required a great deal of flexibility. It finally dawned on me one day that flexibility was a strength of mine, and I should embrace it. I ended up conducting training in all kinds of different spaces with all kinds of different people, learning to maintain composure during technical difficulties, challenging participants, outside distractions, and my own complications behind the scenes. Can you imagine how difficult it would have been to navigate these situations if I insisted on a high level of stability? I probably would have missed a lot of opportunities. I would never have been able to do the jobs I have done if I hadn't been flexible. Lesson learned—before you try to become something you are not, think about whether you might be able to leverage the strengths you have.

Once I focused on consulting full-time, my business grew in ways I never anticipated. I went from being a solopreneur to deploying multinational projects with teams of consultants. This first occurred when I received a call from an international hotel management company that needed management training at all its resorts. Had I simply responded to the need based on my own availability I would have turned down that job, because my schedule was already filled for several months. I am thankful I had the good sense to say yes and find a way to staff it with my friends and industry colleagues. Lesson learned—don't lead with no! Take time to consider the opportunities that come your way, and you may find creative strategies to make them happen.

This client project enabled me to take my business to new levels. I bent over backwards to accommodate the client's needs; when they didn't want to pay a lot up front, I took out a line of credit to fund the project until their payments caught up. Lesson learned—I do not advise putting your own money out there to fund a client project. That decision led to some debt that haunted me for several years.

A few years after the initial large project, I was awarded another contract that was my first seven-figure deal. We were moving into a new house, and this contract made it so much easier to do that. There was just one issue. The signed contract was to be delivered, along with a check for the deposit, the very same day we were closing on our new house. And it never arrived. The client had been a good client for many years and I had no reason to suspect that the contract wouldn't be forthcoming, but suddenly they went completely silent. I sent emails, left voicemails, and received no responses. This went on for four months. This is when I learned the hard way that having a relationship with a single person in a large company is not ideal. What I didn't know at the time was that my client contact was being worked out of her position at the company.

This was excruciating for me. I have literally never seen or heard from this contact again. Upon reflection, I realized how much of my self-worth and feelings of prosperity were wrapped up in this one single client. I vowed to never again have my well-being, whether it be from work or life in general, dependent on one single person. Although I said I had faith in God, I was putting way more faith in this contract than anything else. Eventually her replacement contacted me, and we began doing business together again. The large contract never materialized, and my workload with them was greatly reduced. In hindsight, this enabled me to diversify my business and find other clients, which was a good thing. It also enabled me to renew my faith and trust in the Lord to lead me instead of placing my faith in material things.

I can't overemphasize how upsetting it was when this client just stopped responding. I really want to encourage you—no matter how busy you are, no matter how many emails are in your inbox—to take the time to respond. Even if all you can say is that you will get back to them within a certain number of days, that is something. At least the person knows that they've been heard. I am shocked at the number of people who use their excuse of being too busy as a reason to have very poor manners in the workplace. I think people deserve timely responses. It doesn't mean that you should be chained to your email or your phone 24/7; it is good to set boundaries. But it's always better to set clear expectations about when and how you will respond than to never respond. Bad news rarely gets better by putting off sharing it. I can deal with just about anything, as long as I know where I stand.

Moving on from that, I began to reimagine my business model. One mainstay for training facilitators is the evaluations at the end of each session. I can't imagine how I could have transitioned into a career that required such constant evaluations from others if I had still been paralyzed by other's perceptions of me. I did learn that for many people who work in learning and development, the thrill of the job is about pleasing others—being thought of as a great presenter by everyone you train. I did not like this, and realized I was different. I was much more interested in helping businesses and people get results. Letting go of worrying whether I was pleasing others helped me do a better job, even if this was a lesson that took me decades to fully learn. I was growing in my intellectual humility, or managerial courage, or whatever the en vogue term is for finding my voice, but it still took me years to find that courage on the home front. I still struggled to measure up to everyone else's view of success.

Learning my worth and acknowledging my limits was a continual process. Another friend once told me, as I was stressing out over having too many client commitments and too little time to prepare for them all, "We don't truly know our limits until we reach them." So true! I remember thinking about my hourly rate when I began and wondering if I would ever double it. I thought it seemed arrogant to charge a high rate, and hated when I heard an older consultant, a guy who had been doing this over twenty years, boast in the early 2000s that he "wouldn't get out of bed for less than $5,000 a day." I vowed I would never get to the point of having an overinflated ego. A few years later, to my surprise, I had quadrupled my fees.

Getting to that point was challenging, and I can honestly say I did not raise my rates out of egotism or greed. It was simply a response to a demand for my services. I could work a subcontract job for four full days or work directly for a client for one full day for the same rate. As a consultant, I could book more gigs at cheaper rates or fewer days at higher rates. At the end of the year, the income would be about the same. It was more about the quality of life I wanted to enjoy with my children than anything else. I used to tell people, when asked what I did for a living, that my job was "to make my children think I worked as little as possible."

I learned so many lessons that guided my path over the years, and I would not have been nearly as successful without advisors, mentors, and trusted friends. Surround yourselves with good people and do not try to go it alone! So many women think other women are a threat, and that is very sad to me. I think people either have an abundance mentality or a scarcity mentality. An abundance mentality means that you believe there is enough to go around—enough success, enough work, enough money, enough opportunities, enough love, etc.

A scarcity mentality tends toward the opposite, believing that success, opportunity, money, friendships, and everything else is in finite supply and that there is not enough to go around. I am thankful I have an abundance mentality. It has served me well. You can't always act like you know it all and have everything figured out. That is different from confidence! Per my earlier comments about self-esteem, there is no egotism or arrogance when you "know you're good and wear it well," as the late, great Bob Moawad defined it. People have told me I come off as very confident. The same people have also complimented me on my humanity—being real and not trying to appear that everything is perfect in my world. I am open and vulnerable, and I am also confident and bold. Letting go of the need for absolute perfection has been one of the best gifts I have given myself.

—∽—

"And in the end
the **love**
you take
is equal to
the **love**
you make."

"THE END," THE BEATLES

CHAPTER EIGHT

Collaboration and Authenticity Drive True Success

Despite the pervasive cliché framing workplace goals as "climbing the corporate ladder," a healthy relationship with work doesn't have to involve a quest to reach higher rungs at all. Unfortunately, **Striving Sabrina** has been unable to shed that paradigm, so she prioritizes upward mobility above all else. If, to a hammer, everything looks like a nail, it's also true that to a **Striving Sabrina**, everything looks like a ladder with limited room at the top. If you work with a **Sabrina** and you tend more toward **Camryn** or **Isabella**, you have probably learned to stay out of her way, lest she steamroll you on her way to her ambitious goals.

Driven by a scarcity mentality, **Striving Sabrina** typifies another cliché—"looking out for number one"—and in her tunnel vision often lacks connection to her coworkers or sensitivity about who she might hurt on the way to her goal. She has little time for individuals below her on the ladder, and she only regards those on the same level as competition. Her primary focus is on her superiors, since they are the ones with the power to propel her to the place she most wants to reach. She has convinced herself that her workplace is a game with winners and losers, and she won't entertain the notion that she would find herself on the losing end.

Even if she reaches her goals, the truth is that **Sabrinas** are often the loneliest people in an organization, because they have pitted themselves against those who are supposed to be their teammates. In their laser focus on moving up they sacrifice self-awareness, acting in untrustworthy ways in service to their ambition. The result? Coworkers might not understand or trust **Sabrina,** and they don't appreciate being set up as an opponent in a game they didn't sign up for. Maybe **Sabrina** has put up the walls of always striving for the top because she was passed over in the past and swore she would never miss another opportunity to succeed, or maybe someone taught her that schmoozing higher-ups is the only way to thrive in the workplace. But however **Sabrina** reached this place, her self-centered striving poses a threat to her own well-being and to true unity within her organization.

I recently worked with an incredibly beautiful woman who displayed characteristics of both **Striving Sabrina** and **Perfect Paige.** She was single, perfectly put together, the social butterfly of the office, the party planner extraordinaire, and a hard worker. She always tried to stay above the fray and strived to be credible. She wore her busyness as a sign of pride. She put in a lot of long hours and was the prototype of someone who works hard but doesn't necessarily work smart.

One day, one of our higher-level leaders saw her after hours in her office and he said, "What are you doing here this late?" She said, "Well, I just have so much to do." But he said, "If you stay late like this, people may wonder why you can't get your job done in normal working hours like everyone else." Some people I worked with, like this coworker, always wanted to arrive before and leave after the boss because they thought it would make them look good, like they were the hardest workers. But this habit could work against them, especially if they weren't smart about prioritizing and being strategic in managing up.

This **Sabrina** did get married and had several children. I thought motherhood would mellow my friend, because of my own experience as a mom. I had realized that in motherhood my life was no longer my own, since the needs of my two other humans came first. But I was shocked to see that motherhood did not seem to change this **Striving Sabrina** in the least. She never let on that she might be struggling or overwhelmed, though she continued to work full-time. She handled her children the same way she handled herself, ensuring they were perfectly dressed and coifed, meeting all the right milestones in their development, playing the right sports, and attending the right schools.

Perhaps everything just worked out perfectly for my coworker; she did finally leave her job, but only at the exact time she determined it was financially sound for her to do so. Some **Sabrinas** may just be lucky like that, or maybe they only appear to be, and the realities of their private life are far different than what the rest of the world sees. If the latter is the case, how much energy is someone expending in the quest to appear to "have it all"? And as they climb the ladder of success, how do they know it's leaning against the right wall? **Striving Sabrina** reminds me of a duck, looking so smooth and graceful above the surface of the water and paddling like crazy underneath to try to keep going. Living this way subjects someone to a great deal of stress. It's not enough to keep the facade up at work either—they've got to look like they're the best mom, perfect wife, best parent, best volunteer, and on and on it goes. To show any chinks in their armor would be to admit defeat, and that is not the way **Sabrina** wants to end her competition.

I find it very refreshing how the vulnerability movement has caught on and how people are really trying to celebrate showing up authentically, but unfortunately I don't know that the **Striving Sabrinas** or **Perfect Paiges** of the world will ever get comfortable with that.

Sometimes **Striving Sabrina** lacks the perspective to remove herself from the rat race because she is convinced that scaling the ladder as quickly as possible is the only route to fulfillment. Ashley, who has worked as a general counsel for several different companies, said that she is dismayed when women have such a skewed view of "making it" in life that they pour all of their energy into professional achievement. "I often say, 'Think about what being successful means to you. Is it just money? Is it a title or a corner office? Is it having time to do the things you love?' And I think sometimes women are like robots. They just go. They're looking for the next promotion or the next raise. They forget to get married. They forget to have children. And suddenly they're ten years out, and they've been working fifteen-hour days for ten years, and they realize the clock's ticking. They don't have a life."

Some **Sabrinas** know that they are too driven, but they have found themselves trapped by a workplace culture with upside-down values. Anita felt like she couldn't win in her male-dominated workplace, that she had to strive constantly to gain credibility when it seemed much easier for the men in her organization. If she sent an email at 1 a.m., she said, she faced criticism that she was working too hard. If she chose not to reply to an email outside of office hours, she was told that she wasn't responsive enough. Additionally, she struggled to be in the room where decisions were made because the male managers so often had important discussions on the golf course, or on the hunting trip, or in the cigar lounge. "That's been the hardest thing for me—to get where I need to be, to make it into the inner circle and not be perceived as pushy on my way to get there."

Naomi has faced similarly thorny dynamics in her workplace, she said, striving to excess because it feels like the only way to prove herself. "I am a female in a male-dominated profession, and I constantly come into contact with people who do not think I should be in my profession," she said. "I feel like women have to be more qualified, do the job better, and settle for being paid less and overlooked."

Work environments that are more cutthroat than supportive are breeding grounds for **Sabrina** types, often pitting employees against each other in a faux competition that eliminates the possibility of mutually beneficial collaboration. This environment is particularly problematic when it creates a competition between women who should be lifting each other up instead of trying to push each other off the ladder. Some of our respondents, like Hope, found that this pressure cooker made them less likely to form authentic relationships and more prone to keep striving and looking out for themselves. "It's made me more guarded and careful," she said.

TRAPS: PITFALLS TO AVOID

We have already said that **Sabrinas** can be created by a "me-first" workplace culture, but employees fixated on advancement to the exclusion of everything else can also poison a previously healthy environment. In her hyperfocus on her own ambition, **Striving Sabrina** will inevitably fall into traps that ultimately can diminish both her own work experience and that of the people around her.

One of the most toxic pitfalls often perpetuated by **Sabrina** types, a workplace problem mentioned by a number of our survey respondents, is office gossip. **Sabrina** is certainly not the only type of woman to traffic in gossip, but her tendency to view those around her as threats increases the likelihood that she will tear them down to others. As Abby stated, "There is no place for gossip at work. It will always come back to haunt you." And April, who works in the corporate coaching field, said that she was harmed earlier in her career by nasty gossip in her workplace; it can be difficult to keep your head down and do your work when someone seems to be coordinating a smear campaign against you. "I think it's a way for some women to try and keep the upper hand or undercut someone they think is a threat," she said. "It's happened to me more than once."

Mary, a customer service manager, said she has been bothered by female coworkers who are convinced the boss is playing favorites, so they gossip or act catty to other women in their organization because they believe it will help them get ahead. This behavior often carries a double consequence—it erodes their coworkers' trust and backfires when the boss learns how they have been behaving. "What they don't realize is when they are gossiping or fighting for the boss's attention, they are making themselves look immature and annoying the boss," she said. "I try to stay neutral, but it can be tricky."

Another problematic issue with the culture **Sabrinas** can foster in an organization is an unhealthy spirit of competition, often most intensely with other women. Certainly coworkers do compete in transparent ways sometimes, such as a situation where a promotion is only available to one person on a team. But unity, productivity, and purpose break down on a team when someone, often a **Striving Sabrina**, sets herself up as a competitor in a game that her coworker wasn't even aware she was playing. Listen to Vanessa describe her experience on this hazardous playing field:

"In every company I've worked for, I have had a woman colleague who is trying to compete, but it's so covert," she said. "It's withholding information, it's leaving somebody out of an important conversation, it's not making time to share their knowledge with you so you can then in turn do your job better. I'm perfectly okay with the overt style of competition. If someone wants to race against me, let's go! Right? It's the covert style that I have such a challenge with. And it's just unnecessary. We don't need to be in competition. I feel like it interferes a lot with getting the best work done."

Unfortunately, sometimes the women who need solidarity the most shy away from opportunities to bond with other women. Past offenses, or an "every woman for herself" workplace environment, may have convinced them that opportunity is a scarce commodity, and they must keep their armor on to prove that they can prevail.

Competition goes hand in hand with the comparison trap, because when these women are dissatisfied with their situation as measured against others, they feel the need to strive and surpass. Theodore Roosevelt is credited with saying, "comparison is the thief of joy," and women are especially prone to opening themselves up to that form of burglary.

Mothers compare their children, working mothers compare their ability to keep all the plates spinning, and women in the workplace compare their position or their level of success with other women, often using their perceived insufficiency as fuel for their **Sabrina** tendencies.

Sally has seen the harm of keeping score in this way, she said, and she tries to remind herself that no one knows the whole story about another person's circumstances. "I think that comparing ourselves to others is a major barrier to feeling successful or fulfilled," she said. "I want to be able to be the mom at the field trip, or the mom whose house looks like a Pinterest story. When I am doing well at work, I seem to suffer at home, and when I do well at home, my work suffers. I think that I set unrealistic expectations for myself to be everything for everyone and let myself down the most." Leslie laments women's tendencies to put themselves below others in the comparison game, which is essentially assigning scores to a game in which no one knows the rules. "You make assumptions about other people and other people's lives that might lead you to feel unfulfilled," she said.

In their effort to keep themselves at the forefront, some **Sabrinas** alienate those around them and eliminate the possibility of authentic connection. Charlene had an experience with a manager who drove a wedge between herself and subordinate team members because she thought she had to lead in a forceful, aggressive manner. That supervisor ended up losing her job, but Charlene clearly saw the harm such an approach can have on an organization's culture. "She would tell her staff to be more demanding of my team, and to speak in a more commanding voice to them and me," she said. "Basically you're saying, 'Be ugly. Cut us off. Don't be so polite, don't be friendly.' Because somehow she thought that would make them more powerful. But all it did was make it more difficult for all of us to work together."

TECHNIQUES:
HOW TO SHOW UP EFFECTIVELY

Spend time in self-reflection. If a **Sabrina** takes a break from her climbing long enough to reflect, she might very well find that she is not even confident about her destination. The foundational strategy for converting striving into thriving in the workplace is examining your values, goals, and motives and assessing whether a steamroller approach—taking out others on the way to a perceived pinnacle—is even aligned with who you want to be. It is worthwhile to evaluate the relationships, accomplishments, and culture around you in your organization and ask if things have gotten away from you, if you would be more fulfilled with a pivot toward generosity and collaboration. If you reach the top of the ladder but you leave a pile of bodies in your wake, can that really be considered a successful climb? If **Sabrina** reframes her goals and the means she employs to reach them, she can multiply her impact and her fulfillment at work.

Not everyone finds it easy to evaluate themselves honestly, so a **Sabrina** seeking to change might also want to carefully examine the feedback she gets from coworkers and managers. Consider the green tail principle in this situation; if one person says you have a green tail, they're crazy; if two people say it, they are conspiring against you; but if three people say it, you must check to see if you really have a green tail. You may know for certain you do not have a green tail, but there is a reason people perceive that you do. If your drive to achieve in the workplace is having an adverse effect on those around you, they will start to let you know, and honest acceptance of their views can be a catalyst for improvement.

Adopt an abundance mentality. It's amazing how much more enjoyable a workplace can be when you believe earnestly that there is plenty of success to go around, and even take more interest in the success of others than your own. Those who are inspired to elevate others find that they are elevated too, even if their motivations are purely selfless. And a team builder who exalts in the success of the group realizes that true success is never strictly an individual accomplishment.

Be transparent about your goals. Another strategy for a **Sabrina**, an approach that can help her calibrate her natural desire to succeed with her values and expectations, is to enter a job with clearly stated goals and an open approach to communication with higher-ups. When women are upfront about their hopes for advancement and what it will take to reach them, they are less likely to engage in guerrilla warfare like gossip and over-competitiveness. Anita is always grateful for the employees who understand this coming into a performance review, she said, because she is much better equipped to help those individuals grow. "When I go into reviews, I expect that my direct reports are going to tell me an accurate assessment of what they're enjoying, what they're not enjoying, what stretch goals they have, and what I can be doing better as a leader," she said. "But sometimes I see women who are not assertive enough and not clear about what their dreams or goals are."

Reconsider your view of failure. Professional setbacks are inevitable, but a **Sabrina** who has learned to temper her ambition with healthy expectations can gain a new attitude toward the goals she doesn't meet. When an opportunity doesn't work out, an intriguing question to ask is, "What does this make possible?" The old cliché about closed doors and open windows can prove true for women who move through disappointments with an eye toward a different, and possibly better, path. I have learned that so vividly on my own career journey, as my next step has rarely been the one I would have mapped out for myself, but it always leads me where I need to go. Taylor has realized that refusing to see her work through a scarcity lens makes all the difference, she said, especially when things don't go exactly the way she thought they would. Just as an abundance mentality allows us to envision success for both us and those around us, it also opens up the possibility for success in realms we have never imagined.

"I think what happens is we're very short-sighted," Taylor said. "You know, the opportunity to be promoted is not given to us, or the client who we thought we were going to have a great engagement with changed their mind. But I live by the model that things are always working out for me. So if the client says not now, I go, 'Oh, things are always working out for me.' I look at my calendar and I think, 'Oh, I'm so glad we didn't have that gig at that time.' And when I look back, I think, 'Oh, I was right about that. Things are always working out for me.' But I have had an abundance mentality from the time I started abusiness, even throughout times when there was very little in my bank account and I was in overdraft. I knew it would always come back, and it always did."

—∞—

My Road

Years ago, when my kids were in elementary school, I encountered a situation where a woman had told some complete lies about me, saying I said some things about another woman that I had not ever said. I was really surprised by this and could not figure out why she would make things up to slander me. When I was confronted about what I had supposedly said, I spoke the truth—that I didn't say those things. However, the woman who thought I had been gossiping about her did not believe me. This really bothered me. I have a high need for justice, and I wanted the woman to know I didn't say those things.

My husband advised me to let this go. He rightfully said I couldn't possibly win in this situation, because those two women were close friends and would take each other's sides. I couldn't stand feeling so helpless in defending my honor, but I had to let it go. But it really got to me. I woke up in the middle of the night with a song playing in my head. It was "Voice of Truth" by Casting Crowns. The chorus kept repeating through my mind: "The voice of truth tells me a different story. The voice of truth says do not be afraid. The voice of truth says this is for my glory. Out of all the voices calling out to me, I will choose to listen and believe the voice of truth." I believe that was the Holy Spirit giving me the peace I had prayed for that night as I went to bed. That song kept echoing in my head and a thought came to me: A liar will likely lie to others and the truth will eventually be revealed, but it won't be due to my gossiping.

Several years later, I learned that this same woman who had lied in that situation had a pattern of doing that to others. I do not know the circumstances in her life that might have caused her to do this, but several other false stories fully intended to hurt other people were attributed to her. As the truth came out and more people learned she told stories to hurt other people, I did take comfort in knowing mine was not an isolated incident.

If I told lies, I wouldn't be able to sleep at night because I would have so much trouble trying to keep up with them. I can't imagine how exhausting that might be for someone deep down inside. The key is we need to deal with our stuff. I'm proud of how my kids have dealt with their stuff, and of their resilience. I credit that to situations like this where I tried to model grace in somewhat helpless circumstances. When I had a difficult boss who was making me the scapegoat for his own shortcomings, I realized I needed to stay in my own lane and that the truth would come out eventually. And it did. What you do eventually catches up to you, whether it's good or bad. The voice of truth says do not be afraid. If we can hold on to that voice in the midst of our circumstances, it will give us peace.

My faith has played a huge role in my life. I am not here to preach, but I am here to share what has worked for me and given me strength to press forward in tough times and when faced with challenging decisions. Having the perspective of a higher power guiding my path centered me and helped me with the one most important guiding principle in my life—maintaining hope! That constant hope and expectation provided invaluable perspective. When things were bad, I hung on to the hope that "this too shall pass," a phrase I have repeated to my children hundreds of times as well. Also, living with the promise of eternal life based on my spiritual beliefs has helped me aim for eternal things and not worldly possessions. Don't get me wrong—I love a great designer purse and a nice car as much as anyone, but I do not believe my worth or significance is tied to these things.

One of my absolute favorite verses for dealing with challenges is Romans 5:1-5. You can look it up, but I like the 1984 NIV version wording the best: "Therefore, since we have been justified through faith, we have peace with God through our Lord Jesus Christ, through whom we have gained access by faith into this grace in which we now stand. And we rejoice in the hope of the glory of God. Not only so, but we also rejoice in our sufferings, because we know that suffering produces perseverance; perseverance, character; and character, hope. And hope does not disappoint us, because God has poured out his love into our hearts by the Holy Spirit, whom he has given us." How great is that? I like to think this is the first definition of resilience, a term so popular in today's business vernacular. Whether you are a Christian or not, I think we can all agree that finding a way to embrace your challenges, persevere through them, build character, and maintain hope is a fantastic way to have staying power in this world. When I have wondered where my next job or next dollar is coming from, I have seen my prayers answered in ways I never imagined.

There was a time when I had taken a lot of time off due to some personal circumstances, and I literally wondered how I would pay the bills. The next day I received a call from a Christian radio station (how ironic is that?) who needed some help with business strategy and staff teambuilding. Prayer answered. This is why I do not believe there are coincidences in our lives. I believe everything is divinely orchestrated. We don't always understand why or how, and prayers are not always answered in our timing or in the ways we want them to be, but there is a higher power in control. Of this I am fully confident.

By the way, I did not become a Christian based on religious sacraments. I was confirmed and said all the right things, professing to believe the Lord was my savior. But saying so did not make me feel it in my heart. It wasn't until I experienced a bad breakup and felt truly hopeless and helpless that my faith became personal. Thanks to some amazing friends who helped me through that bad situation, and prayers that made my faith personal, my life was truly changed. I think it is easy to say you are a believer, or that you are not, but have you ever put your faith to the test? When we are at our lowest point and don't know where to turn, that is the gap where our faith can step in.

I don't know about you, but when my life is at its worst, that is when my prayer life is at its best. I am not trying to force anything on anyone. I am simply saying my faith is something that has consistently helped me in my journey. It is unfortunate how many times I have heard someone say they were turned off by Christians for one reason or another. Typically, it's because someone tried to force it upon you, used their faith as a thinly veiled excuse to judge or condemn you, or something along those lines. I would encourage you (and them) to look at the book of James. There is a great deal written about mere mortals like us judging one another, and I, for one, am thankful it is not up to me to judge and mete out justice for our sins here on earth.

If I could just say one thing to those of you who are non-believers it would be this: Don't let one situation or person make your faith decision for you. Do the research (I am a fan of the book *The Case for Christ*, by Lee Strobel) and decide for yourself whether you believe or not. We are saved by the grace of God alone (Ephesians 2:8-9). We can't do enough to earn it, and it is not about being sinless or a good person. It is not something for us to boast about. It is a gift that provides eternal life, and I love the prospect of that! It is never too late, until the moment you die, and there is nothing you have done or could do that would separate you from God. I believe our God is a God of love, who wants to welcome each of us into his kingdom. Regardless of your spiritual beliefs, it is my belief that we are called to love one another, and this world needs more love, less judgment, and less hate. We do not have to believe the same things or worship the same God to treat each other with caring, kindness, and mutual respect.

I was so very thankful to be rooted in my faith, since it was about to be tested in a huge way. Balancing our two-career family was quite difficult. Our priorities were based on which one of us made the most money, but that should not have been our driving factor. I learned this the hard way.

My career took a back seat to my husband's, since he made more money and seemed to have a higher trajectory. Looking back, I suppose I might have made a different decision if I knew then what I know now. But you can't spend too much time looking back at what might have been. Look back just long enough to learn the lessons you can, but then spend your time looking forward. Life is like driving a car—as you move forward your windshield is very large, showing you what is on the horizon. Your rearview mirror is small. It's large enough to illuminate what is behind you, but it's smaller because you need to focus mostly on what is ahead. My marriage was in trouble for years, make that more than a decade, before it finally ended. I was miserable for a long time, and to be fair, he might have been too. There were some things my husband never mentioned when we were dating—things like mental health issues and unresolved family-of-origin dynamics that really affected our relationship.

This is not a tell-all book, and I do not want to trash my ex-husband. He is the father of my children, and we were together for many years. But in the spirit of sharing what I have learned, I will say please, please deal with your stuff! We all have stuff! Remember, you can either deal with it, or deal with the consequences of not dealing with it. And as important as it is and was for me to deal with my stuff, none of us can deal with other people's stuff. And we cannot make them deal with their stuff no matter how we try.

As I previously mentioned, I had quite an aversion to quitting or failing, so I never, ever would have foreseen myself getting divorced. Based on what I have shared so far, you can probably guess that I would have been mortified at the thought of breaking an engagement or calling it quits in my marriage. What would people think? How would I move forward? What if I never found love again? I hope you have never suffered through these same thoughts. But if you have, I would say—LET IT GO! Over the years I had several friends who went through relationship challenges—marital trials, divorce, or losing their spouse. I learned something from each of these situations, but one in particular stood out to me.

About a year before my own divorce, I learned that a dear friend of mine and her husband planned to divorce. I wasn't sure how I felt about it. I asked her if they'd tried counseling, if she was certain this was the best plan, and I probably came off as judgmental. Perhaps I was projecting my own issues onto her. My husband and I were so distant from one another that I didn't feel I knew him anymore, but I didn't spend much time thinking about it. Rather, I threw myself into my work and stayed busy with the kids. We had been married over twenty years, and I thought this was just how marriage was going to be. While it was less than ideal, it was familiar and somewhat comfortable. And I didn't fail at things, so why spend time worrying about it?

My friend who was headed toward divorce spent a lot of time considering how to separate. This type of consideration had its merits, to be sure, but I found myself thinking she should just do it already, which probably says more about my own impatience than her judgment. I remember telling her I thought she needed to care less about what the neighbors thought and just focus on helping her children deal with the situation. I had no idea at that time just how profound this observation would be or the stark reality I would soon face as I had to take my own advice.

I will never forget the precise date and time I learned of my husband's affair. He had been acting very strange for months, but I had no idea what was coming next. He was not very social, so the thought of him having an affair with a real live person was a distant worry. I'd have sooner expected him to be on an online site since he spent countless hours on his computer, preferring that to spending time with people. One night, we went to bed after a disagreement, and he awoke at about 4 a.m. like he usually did. The man barely slept, but that was only one of the unusual behaviors he had adopted over the past several months. About 5:30 am, I awoke from a dream with a start. I had just dreamed that he was having an affair. I realized I was alone in bed, and I spent the next three hours tossing and turning trying to go back to sleep and erase the memory of that dream.

At about 8:30 he came back into the bedroom to ask if I wanted to go to church, since it was Sunday. I told him I was tired because I'd had a bad dream and had not been able to get back to sleep or get it out of my head. Then I further explained that I'd dreamed he was having an affair. The expression on his face changed and he looked like he'd seen a ghost. I then said, "and you aren't saying anything right now to make me think it isn't true." He then came in, sat down on the bed, and started to spill his guts. Yes, he was having an affair.… he really liked her.… he didn't want to tell me about it because he wasn't sure where it was going, but he'd like to spend more time with her. The weirdest part is that I was strangely calm the entire time. I spoke in a quiet measured tone and said I thought he should do just that—leave the house and spend more time with her. But I had one request—that he would tell our children the truth about his affair. They were fourteen and sixteen at the time, and I felt they could handle the truth. I didn't want him to try to say we were just unhappy or grew apart or anything like that. I wanted them to know he was having an affair. Four days later I hired an attorney, which absolutely shocked him.

I was quite stunned and sad, but my most prevalent emotion was anger. I was angry that after all I felt he put me through, after how miserable I had been, that he had done this. I am certain I made mistakes during that time. It was quite challenging to navigate the situation with the kids and with others. I take it as a bit of a compliment that many of my closest friends and family members had no idea how miserable I had been. I suppose that means I did not complain about my marriage. But when I finally laid it out there and they knew all that the kids and I had endured, they were nothing short of amazing. There was no judgment, at least by the people who mattered most in my life. There was no shame. There was simply love, acceptance, and true friendship.

Oh, how I leaned on people over the months that followed. My brother drove me to the appointment with the attorney when I wasn't strong enough to drive myself (dissolving into a puddle of tears while driving on Houston freeways was not a good prospect!). My key employee took the reins of my business, ensuring my service to clients was uninterrupted, even finding others to step in for me so I didn't have to worry about being in front of my clients. My friends lent an ear and a shoulder to cry on. My kids and I found solace at church, and the youth ministers poured into them to provide them support as well. We also found therapists who helped us deal with all the aspects of this situation.

My faith was tested, and the Lord sustained me. There is only one way I can explain how I came to learn of my husband's affair. It was the Holy Spirit working in this situation. How else can I explain that I had this dream, remained so calm, and knew how to proceed when my world was falling apart? And all the things I had said to my friend came back to me. I couldn't worry about what others thought of me or of this situation. Were there people who judged me? Indeed, I am certain there were. I even had my family doctor (who quickly became my ex-family doctor!) lecture me that it was my duty to stay wed to my husband. But those people did not matter. I could no longer hang on to worrying about what people thought of me. I had to prioritize my children's and my own well-being. I had to embrace my failings and imperfections and learn how to rebound from them. And this has led to greater fulfillment, happiness, and love than I have ever known! I couldn't imagine how my life would change.

—m—

I can see,
it took so long
just to realize
I'm much too strong
not to compromise

Now I see what I am is holding me down
I'll turn it around
Oh, yes I will

"DON'T LOOK BACK," BOSTON

CHAPTER NINE

A View from the Other Side

Our deep dive into the seven archetypes—what characterizes each, what leads each type to get stuck, and the best path to freedom from those traps—relied on my own experiences and on wisdom from the dozens of women who contributed their voices to this book. But even though this book is for and mostly by women, we did not want to miss the opportunity to have some men share their perspectives on the landscape of today's workplace.

A healthy organization is never a battle of the sexes; it is made up of women and men all doing their best to listen, collaborate, and grow and to navigate any tension that might arise because of their differences. With that understanding, I spent time talking to a handful of men in various business leadership roles about how they view the balancing act facing women and how they seek to keep women from getting stuck.

As they considered the roles women play in and out of the office, most of the men I interviewed acknowledged that women carry an outsized portion of the load. Raymond, the owner of a small marketing company, was raised by a single mother trying to manage every aspect of both her work and her home life, and in his childhood and from his professional vantage point as an adult, he has noticed that societal pressures tilt the burden toward the woman in virtually every situation.

"When you asked me about the roles and which are easier for women, my first thought is that none of these things are easier for women than for men, because of the way society is structured, you know?" he said. "Society imposes that, but because we've grown up in the world, we also tend to believe those things ourselves. I don't think being a leader is easier for a woman than for a man. I don't think being a parent is easier for a woman than for a man. I don't think being an employee is easier; I don't think being a caregiver is easier. It just sucks to say it, but yeah."

Several of our interviewees acknowledged the innate differences between men and women, such as the more nurturing tendencies of most women, and traced those different qualities to the imbalance between the loads carried by working women and working men. David, who is a father and grandfather as well as a sales executive, believes because women are typically more empathetic they are better suited to take the lead as caregivers and as the leaders of families. "I just don't think we're equipped to do as good a job in those areas," he said. "If empathy is a critical value in terms of creating that culture, then I think women are better equipped."

Carter, a man in his twenties who works for a larger multinational company, believes that perspectives on gender differences are often divided between those who seek to erase all variations between men and women and those who refuse to see past the most traditional views of men's and women's roles. "I think some people lack a holistic approach, and focus on celebrating the differences between sexes to a fault, and I think that feminists tend to lack respect for these differences," he said. "We should celebrate femininity and acknowledge the areas that we're failing to do so without devaluing masculinity."

Appreciating the different strengths women bring to the table can help managers find the optimal workplace role for the women in their organization, the men we interviewed said. Patrick, who works in finance, said that women excel when it comes to mentoring younger employees, both because they tend to be more naturally empathetic and because they have often been through challenges and they understand how to help others navigate the difficulties that arise. "The people who have mentored me have been predominantly women, and those have been the better mentors to me," Patrick said. "Maybe it's because there's a certain innate sense built in, that women have had it tougher coming up and they want to make it better for the next person."

Our male respondents also had insight about the ways women in their organizations make things more difficult for themselves. Blake has witnessed situations where women let their emotions get the best of them and react instead of preparing a more measured response, he said, and in his experience women can be quicker to let stressful situations overwhelm them. "They may snap at someone," he said. "They may be short. They may miss deadlines, and the rest of the group will not think very highly of them." This downward spiral can fracture the relationships on a team, he said, all sparked because the woman in question didn't feel comfortable telling a manager that she was overloaded and working to solve the problem.

When Daniel was twenty-five, he was working as a credentialed actuary in a highly professional setting when a forty-year-old coworker started yelling at him one day in her office. Daniel didn't see a cause for her extreme anger, and when word got around about her behavior, the woman was reprimanded. "The next day she apologized and said that sometimes she had trouble controlling her emotions at certain times of the month," he said. "I told her I did not like being yelled at for any undeserved reason." Daniel's perspective of this experience is an important reminder that women should never use hormones or any other circumstances as an excuse to let their emotions run rampant. (Neither should men, for that matter!)

Blake is aware that some of his female coworkers are trying fruitlessly to keep too many balls in the air, he said, either because they are overextended or because a crisis at home is pulling their attention. His is a collaborative, understanding workplace, he said, but he sees those women putting on a brave face and powering through instead of admitting that they could use a hand from the team. "Look for help," he said. "Build relationships with your coworkers and your boss and let them in a little bit to your life, and they'll help you on the journey. People generally want to help one another, and I'm sure the favor will be returned on the other side. Open yourself up, so that people know what you're going through."

Our respondents agreed that women bring valuable interpersonal skills into the workplace that can teach men how to be more vulnerable and empathetic, but at times a man's distinct way of seeing a situation can also sharpen a female coworker. Patrick walked through an example of this recently at his company, when he had a conversation with a woman partner in his firm who was experiencing a conflict with an employee. The woman wanted to call the employee in question right away and talk through everything again, but Patrick felt that such an immediate debrief would not be in anyone's best interest. Because of the circumstances of their company and that employee's immediate responsibilities, he advised her to wait on the conversation and to let the situation simmer over the weekend.

"The main approach was, 'Don't go call him again. Debrief it next week,'" Patrick said. "And she said that was really helpful, because that was exactly what she was about to do and it wouldn't have changed anything. Sometimes women should think more like a man in a given situation. But obviously, there are far more times when I would advise men, 'Hey, you need to think more like a woman would in this case.' At times the advice I have is to not take things personally, or to just compartmentalize tasks versus people matters. Maybe it's stereotypical, but I think men in general, the way their brains are wired, they have an easier time compartmentalizing than women."

We have already talked about how women can be overly competitive, and even cruel, to other women in the workplace. Blake said that he has noticed this "mean girls" phenomenon and how it creates the unfortunate dynamic of women limiting each other's professional growth. A small group of women in his organization created a clique of sorts, and while they weren't overtly unkind, they were also closed to letting anyone new in. Eventually one of the most entrenched members of the group moved on to another job, and the culture improved, but that episode made Blake feel that managers should intervene more intentionally when they feel that bad attitudes, or exclusionary friendships, are eroding a company's collaborative environment.

"You just have to know that it's happening and make sure it's not hurting the rest of the organization and the people in it," he said. "At the time, I didn't take the approach that I'm going to nip this in the bud and tell them that it's unacceptable." Now Blake tries to incorporate themes of inclusion into his team meetings, he said, reminding employees how important it is to bring newcomers, or those who aren't as quick to form relationships, into the community. It isn't all that different from the way parents encourage their children to seek out the child sitting alone at lunch and invite her to join their table.

As they have observed gender differences in the workplace and sought to make the path less hazardous for women trying to thrive, the men we talked with also shared some thoughts about how they could lead women more effectively. In David's opinion, a key first step is crafting a diverse leadership team that can represent the interests of all types of employees. He acknowledges people's natural tendencies to fill their team with individuals who are similar to them, a temptation that should be avoided to create room for all types to thrive. "Historically men have hired other men that look like us, talk like us, and think like us, and it's a mistake," he said. "Now I think some of the women in our organization, as leaders, they have brought in new employees that all look and sound the same too. I see that and I think, 'Wow, let's do a better job of building a diverse team, encouraging each person where they're strong, and then utilizing those strengths.'"

Patrick has found it easier to cultivate an attitude of empathy toward the woman in his company as he has watched his own wife balance the myriad demands of home and work, he said. He encourages other male managers to ask women what their struggles are and how they can better be supported in their juggling efforts. "Men need to be comfortable getting into the weeds of what your women colleagues are going through," he said. "You won't have all the answers, but be comfortable with listening, with understanding that you're not going to get it, but you can still listen and support."

Having placed a priority on hiring a wide range of people for his company's leadership team, Raymond has daily opportunities to practice relating well to employees of different genders, races, and backgrounds. He can sum up his approach to the people in his small company simply in two words: "Hold space." For example, in the midst of a virtual meeting with managers, he might notice one woman, perhaps with **Invisible Isabella** tendencies, who repeatedly gets interrupted when she tries to speak.

"I've learned to say, 'Hold on a second, Maddie? Did you have something you wanted to say?' Just slow it down and give people the floor. Use your power to grab power away from other people to give it to somebody else. You can also hold space when somebody is repeating something that somebody else just said, and you can be like, 'That's exactly what she just said.' That's a good thing that men can do."

Men can also show sensitivity to the women in their workplace by being aware of their body language, particularly in tense discussions with women. Men may unintentionally be perceived as intimidating or patronizing due to their stature. Daniel was working as a math teacher when he got into a discussion with a fellow teacher, a woman who was petite. At one point, as they talked through a disagreement, Daniel stood up because it was more comfortable to him. He found out later from another coworker that the woman believed he was using his height to intimidate her. "Of course that was never my intent, and I can't help it that I'm tall, but I have since kept that female perspective in mind when dealing with women at work," he said.

Raymond considers himself a relational leader, placing people above processes, and he is sure that his upbringing with a "rockstar single mother" has helped him develop empathy for the working women in his company. "I can relate to people really well, and I can really dig in and have conversations about tough things and not take it personally," he said. "I feel good in that regard, but where it's been challenging for me is that I want everything to be great, and when it's not great, I feel guilt. I have fear that we're not living up to what the women really want or need. I'm always kind of grappling with, 'Are we doing enough?'"

Inspired by Kim Scott's book *Radical Candor*, Raymond tries to intentionally create a better work environment for women by urging them to speak out about what they need, and he has also tried to promote qualified women to positions that they are clearly gifted for, even if they don't check every box on the job description. Recently he promoted a female employee to a director's role in digital content even though she wasn't well-versed in search engine optimization. The woman assumed that knowledge gap would disqualify her, but Raymond knew that she had the key intangibles for the position and the ability to catch up quickly on the things she didn't yet understand.

"I told her, 'I don't care that you don't know that.' I put her in that position and she's just rocking it. Stop thinking that you need to have all of the things to be able to take on work and get yourself into projects that you want to take on. Ask for it, even if you're not ready. I try to help women see that in themselves, to be that advocate for them."

My Road

Along the way, my husband did attempt to reconcile, once he lost his job and the affair had faded a bit. The thought of reconciling made me sick to my stomach. That should have told me something, but of course, not being a quitter, I gave it a try. Ultimately, what I finally said to him as my reason for divorcing was this: The very things that most people said were my greatest strengths and gifts were things he disliked and resented about me. How were we ever going to be happy in that situation?

I am thankful my therapist poured truth into me, which I will share with you in the hopes it will inspire you. She said I deserve to be cherished. That word has stuck with me ever since. Cherished. Not just given the leftover crumbs he has once he's dealt with everything else in his life. That was pretty much what was missing from my marriage. When one person is not feeling good about himself or herself, it is tough for them to love and cherish another person. Again, deal with your stuff, and realize you are enough! When I told my therapist my husband had been going through a bad time for years before the affair and that I no longer even recognized the man I married, she said that he also dragged me down with him. That was absolutely true, and it took time and effort, along with the grace of God, to separate myself from him.

I focused a great deal that year on getting the kids through the worst times we'd ever known. Another lesson learned—never, ever say nothing will change when you split up. My ex tried to say that, and I knew it wasn't correct. Everything changed. I knew I would need to return to full-time work to get benefits. We would live in two places, and the kids would need to visit both. Financially, everything would change. And most certainly, the kids' perspective on many things would change as well. Not all the changes were bad, and in fact, in time I realized that many of the changes were for the better.

Over the years I had been approached a few times by people who wanted to acquire my company. Once I knew the divorce was coming, I chose to make that happen. In this process, I learned a lot, much of it the hard way. I found that people tend to make their companies sound better than they are. The first time a company brought me an offer that was too good to be true, I was able to walk away from the deal, although it cost me a lot of money in attorney fees to do so. It was worth it to dodge a bullet. But the second time, I was not so fortunate. I was eager to get into a more stable work arrangement to support myself, so I went through with the deal. I accepted a lower compensation level with the promise of getting significant bonuses on the work I sold for the new company. Suffice it to say, even if you get something in writing, if the person on the other end of the deal is a narcissist with significant financial issues well hidden beneath a seemingly wealthy, opulent lifestyle, the deal will not be worth the paper it is printed on. After a couple of years of broken promises, the best thing I could do was cut my losses and move on. That is when I rejoined corporate America in the role where I would spend seven great years.

Meanwhile, my therapist was encouraging me to date. I did not think the timing was good. My kids were in high school, and wouldn't it be easier to just put that off until they were out of the house? She talked me into setting up an online dating profile, and I decided to give it a try. It had been twenty-seven years since I'd dated and I had no idea what to do! But slowly I figured out how to date in the age of online apps and texting, and ultimately it led me to meet my husband! I believe there was some divine intervention again in this situation.

I had been out with a guy from Iowa a few times and went onto the dating app to look up something about him. I laugh when I tell people the dating app was a lot like shopping on Amazon. I received an ad that said if I liked Iowa Guy #1, I might also like this other guy from Iowa. That guy was Eric. I clicked on his profile and looked him over. We would not have paired up automatically since he was outside a few of my settings—I wanted a guy within five years of my age, and he was five-and-a-half years older than me. But I thought he was cute.

I saw a photo of his daughter who played volleyball at the university my son was planning to attend. Most of the time on these apps, the guys would comment about your looks or say something flirtatious. And I always waited for the guy to make the first move! But I went out on a limb and commented about how cool it was that she played D1 college volleyball since my daughter was also a volleyball player and my son wanted to attend the same school. There was nothing flirtatious about my comments. A few days later I decided to take a break from the dating scene. I hadn't really met anyone I felt too strongly about, and thought it was a distraction I didn't need. I cancelled my dating app membership so it would expire at the end of the month. Two weeks went by and just when I least expected it, I received a reply from him. Thankfully, I still had access to my app, or I would never have received it.

Out of darkness, pain, and loss can come amazing light and love. It is our job to keep hoping and persevering! And if you doubt whether it can work out, just look at me. I was in a difficult work situation and had kids in high school—wise enough to know about the dating scene and just aware enough to be completely mortified at the thought of their mom dating. I was not at my ideal weight, or looking perfect, but I put myself out there anyway. I am so glad I did, not only for the obvious reason that I found Eric, but for another reason too.

In early 2020, out of the blue, after having a routine mammogram I learned I had breast cancer. It was early stage, but there were two different forms of it, and one was aggressive (it's never good when your type of cancer has the word "invasive" in it). So, surgery was scheduled, and radiation would follow. (Little did I know that my surgery in March would coincide with the world shutting down for the pandemic.) At first it was difficult for me to talk about, because the tumor was just under my nipple. I had no evident lump, no family history, and was considered low-risk, but I got breast cancer anyway. Because it was in my nipple-areolar complex (NAC), the surgeon advised that I have a lumpectomy, with the objective of saving my nipple. Unfortunately, they had to remove much more tissue than expected, and could not save my nipple. They did get it all, and that was most important, but it really bothered me to be missing a nipple. Also, what was supposed to be a lumpectomy with a small two-inch scar became a full reconstruction.

This wasn't the type of reconstruction most people think of after a mastectomy. I had a reduction of sorts, reconstructing the breast with the tumor after removing a great deal of tissue. Then the other breast was reconstructed to be similar in size. (Fun fact—they made the other breast thirty percent smaller than the one with the tumor, since radiation would shrink that breast by thirty percent.) Also, three lymph nodes under my arm were removed, and the cancer had not spread to them, thank the Lord. I had twenty-nine inches of incisions, and it was a far more extensive recovery than first thought. Why am I telling you all this detail? Because I am so thankful I had Eric in my life when this happened. First, I am thankful that he loves me so well. He told me he didn't marry me for my breasts and did not care at all that I only had one nipple and scars all over. Although that was exactly what I needed to hear, I still went through a bit of a mourning process, mourning the loss of a bit of my identity as a woman. The very same breasts that fed my children were now scarred and deformed.

Over time I got more comfortable sharing this story because it is an example of all the myriad decisions cancer patients must make quickly. I even got a tattoo of my nipple! The doctor wanted to actually reconstruct my nipple from the other nipple, but I declined that procedure. Now, the scars have faded and I can look in the mirror without being sad. I even joke with Eric that my theme song is "One Headlight" by Jakob Dylan (get it?!?). But my body will never be the same. My tumor was receptive to both progesterone and estrogen, which means those hormones make it grow. This means it is easier to successfully treat, but it also means I cannot take estrogen. Since I was fifty-one when this happened, I was going through menopause, and would love to have had some estrogen to ease my symptoms. Had I waited to find love, with scarred breasts and menopausal symptoms, I doubt I ever would have. So my story is just more evidence to just do it, and don't wait!

I know many people who have had serious health problems like cancer and opted to keep it private. That is a personal choice, but I will say that by opening up about my cancer and my divorce, I have found tremendous comfort in knowing people are praying for me and care about me. I have also found that it helps me connect with others who are going through trials.

—◊—

Every long lost dream led me to where you are

Others who broke my heart, they were like Northern stars

Pointing me on my way into your loving arms

This much I know is true

That God blessed the broken road, That led me straight to you.

"BLESS THE BROKEN ROAD," BY RASCAL FLATTS

CHAPTER TEN

The Second Act

So what do I say in the final chapter? It feels so...final! And I am definitely not finished yet. I would like to close by sharing what has been different for me in the past few years. I never fully grasped the difference that finding love again would make in my life. I don't think I truly understood what true love was. I first fell in love at sixteen, and it was wonderful! I will never forget my first love, but it was really different then, being young and having to grow up and find my way in life. Ultimately, that relationship was not meant to be. I found love again with the man who eventually became my first husband and the father of my children. The best word I would use to describe it was safe. There was attraction, and ultimately the thought of being with him the rest of my life was less scary than the thought of being without him. And I don't doubt there was love there.

But this is different. The love I have for Eric is like nothing I have ever experienced before. There's of course the physical attraction, which is wonderful. But it is everything else too. I fully and completely trust him, and he trusts me. We finish each other's sentences. We never, ever run out of things to talk about. We are completely goofy together and find each other's silly antics and jokes endlessly funny. We tell each other everything. I even tell him my weight, which previously was my most closely guarded secret! I know he wants great things for me, and I want the best for him, too. He is my greatest cheerleader and I am his. I have laughed and smiled more in the years since I met Eric than I ever did in my life up to that point. People tell us they can feel how much in love we are just being around us. I realize I may be nauseating some of you, and I apologize, but I don't know any other way to describe this intense love. I literally do not want to ever imagine life without him. And I would have never known this kind of love had I not endured some tough things to get here.

If you have love like that, I am very happy for you. If you do not, consider whether there might be a way for you to discover it. Maybe your path will not involve the love of a significant other. But who surrounds you? Who are your cheerleaders, your confidants, your true friends? Do you have a spiritual foundation or belief in some higher power, some force for good? I believe Abraham Lincoln had it right when he said, "Most folks are as happy as they make up their minds to be." There are very few times in my life when, looking back, I would say I was unhappy. But I didn't know what I didn't know. True happiness is such a different feeling, and I am so very thankful to be experiencing it. Reflect on what makes you happy and brings you joy, and understand what saps your energy.

After I met Eric, I still had my share of challenges. But knowing there's a person in my corner, someone who makes the rough days bearable and the good days better, makes a huge difference. I no longer feel like my future and well-being are dependent on my performance. In my previous job, this looked like getting more comfortable in leadership, finding my voice, and worrying less. I gained confidence, not just in my abilities at work, but in my worth as a person. Having someone who loves me just the way I am made me slowly realize I am okay right now. Eric and I, once married, enjoyed our life as empty nesters, purchasing and furnishing our first home together, and planning for our future. The kids were doing well most of the time, and truly becoming independent adults. Yes, we had the pandemic, and Eric and I both had our health challenges, but we were really enjoying our life together.

I still strived to be "the best" at work. Titles mattered there, and most of my peers were VPs. I wanted to work my way up to a VP level as well. As a consultant I had worked for so many years with executives, and being able to say I could function well in that role myself was important to me. It felt like it would be a full-circle moment to be able to move from the outside, as a consultant, to a corporate executive on the inside. And I did it, and I was proud. The time I was in that role was fulfilling for many reasons. I had finally built a team after being the only employee in my business area when I started. I saw several programs my team had been working toward come to fruition, and I received accolades for my work. I was traveling more than ever before, but I liked the travel, and the work. Life was good! My son was thriving at work, living a good life fully "adulting," and my daughter was about to follow suit, graduating from college and moving into her first full-time job. I had been fortunate enough to earn good money in those years as well. I was able to pay off my kids' college educations, their cars, and more.

The funny thing was that in the midst of all the good stuff, my body was sending me some strange signals that it was not as happy as the rest of me! Shortly after my breast cancer in 2020, I had a few other medical issues crop up. My oncologist put me on an aromatase inhibitor, which is basically a low-dose chemotherapy pill, typically taken for five years after breast cancer to minimize the chances of recurrence. I began to have severe shortness of breath and ended up in the ER. The doctor stopped the medicine and checked me for a pulmonary embolism and some other issues. Thankfully, all my tests were negative, but I stopped taking that chemo pill.

Shortly after that, one of my cornea transplants failed. The doctors don't know why it happened, but think it may have been due to the radiation treatment I received. So, in the midst of the pandemic lockdown, I had my third transplant. It went well, and the treatment had come a long way since my first two were done. I had a different procedure with a shorter recovery time and no need to wear a patch during the day! I was thrilled, until about a month later when the doctor took the stitches out and I could not see at all. Apparently the procedure had not worked. Less than two months later I had another transplant in that eye, my fourth overall. It was successful and I was thankful!

About six months later I had a symmetry procedure, which is a fancy term for surgery to make my breasts the same size. Fun fact: symmetry procedures are covered for the life of the patient after initial breast cancer surgery. Radiation can shrink your remaining breast tissue by about thirty percent, so even though the plastic surgeon had tried to account for that, my breasts were uneven. The day before surgery, while doing routine bloodwork, I was given a test to check my A1c. I was shocked when I was told I was diabetic. Yet another medical issue had reared its ugly head. I proceeded with surgery and then began tackling diabetes. Thankfully it was relatively mild, and I have been able to control it well. A few months later, my oncologist decided to once again put me on the aromatase inhibitor, since it would really help to minimize the chances of breast cancer recurrence.

All was okay, but when I went to the cornea specialist a month later, I learned my body was rejecting my new cornea transplant. Thankfully, with some special eye drops, the rejection was reversed. The cornea specialist and oncologist determined that although they didn't know for sure, it was possible the aromatase inhibitor might have caused the cornea rejection, so I was off that medicine again, this time permanently. Being the world-class worrier I am, I was concerned that my odds of getting breast cancer again went way up, somewhere around twenty-five percent, but my daughter reminded me that meant I still have a seventy-five percent chance of not getting it. I was navigating these medical ups and downs while working a demanding job, and I am so very thankful I had a fantastic boss who gave me the latitude to get to all these doctors' appointments. She knew I would still put in the hours to get my job done, and then some, being the type-A workaholic I was.

In 2022, when I was working really hard, I went to the doctor for a routine checkup and discovered I had developed high blood pressure. I had been on seven trips in four weeks and my body was exhausted. It was then when I told my boss I thought my body was starting to give me some clear signals that I just could not keep up the pace I had been setting lately. I think that was the beginning of the end of my corporate role, although I didn't know it at the time.

So I needed to give my body a rest, to stop burning the candle at both ends. I needed to make better choices about exercise, food, sleep, and overall health. And it was getting to the point where putting everything and everyone else before myself was taking a severe toll. I have finally started listening to my body and wish it hadn't taken me so long. I hope reading my story will inspire you to take time for self-care and wellness. You are far better able to play all the roles in your life when you are well. I am a slow learner when it comes to this. Don't make the same mistakes I did!

When I left my last job, I felt, for the first time in my adult life, like I could take time to reflect on what I really wanted to do next. I prayed that the Lord would illuminate my path. I had often prayed this prayer, but it was different this time. This time, I did not have a clue where I was headed. I spoke with my favorite former professor about possibly getting my PhD in organizational psychology or something similar. He told me with my real-world experience I did not need academic degrees to be credible. I met with a friend of mine who is an expert in organizational coaching to see if I should go down that path. That led to a wonderful part-time coaching opportunity that I have really enjoyed. I expect I will do more of that in the future, but that alone did not lead to my full-time career path.

A few colleagues of mine who had developed successful consulting practices and were ready to retire spoke with me about purchasing their learning and development companies. I thought about it and did deliver some leadership development training like I used to facilitate. But I noticed something: I didn't enjoy it nearly as much as I used to. The fire was gone, so that probably wasn't the path for me. I had a few interviews for corporate roles, one of which sounded great.

At first I did not want to return to a corporate position, but the more I thought about it and the security it provided, the more it seemed like the right move. I was so sure that was the next step for me that I put all other plans on hold to pursue that opportunity. All signs were pointing toward me getting the role, and I just knew that was where the Lord was leading me. And then that opportunity stagnated over several months and ultimately the role was eliminated, so there was no job to get! I interviewed for a few more roles, but none seemed like the right fit or got me excited at all about going back to a full-time job.

As some doors have closed, others have opened, and it has been so exciting to see where this journey will take me. Have you ever taken steps forward in faith without truly knowing where your path was leading? That is my life right now. I have said for nearly twenty years that my dream was to do public speaking. In fact, that is why I wanted to write this book. I thought it would help me hone my message for future public speaking engagements. Except for those months when I thought I would be going back to a corporate role, I have been working on this book and considering how I might launch a public speaking career since I left my last job.

It is uncanny how many connection points have come about along this journey. I interviewed a long-time friend and colleague in California for this book, and she in turn introduced me to several other working women in her network, many of whom I also interviewed. In one interview, I shared with a woman I had just met that I wanted to do public speaking and that I wanted to get some coaching, but I didn't know a speaker coach. This woman told me about a speaker coach she followed on LinkedIn, and

I began following that coach as well. That led me to joining a twelve-week speakers academy. I went from wondering if and how I might make a go of this speaking thing to being certain it is my calling. I am now engaged with the leadership coach, who is publishing this book, and I hope you will see me on a big stage soon!

Moving forward in faith does not mean staying idle. It means that you just take the next step, even if you don't know where the path is leading you. Giving up and being open to the possibilities that lie before me is so exciting and rewarding. I often say that although I don't know what is in my future, I know who holds the future in His hands. I often tell my kids to stop worrying about what could be ahead of them and simply take the next step. Now, it is my turn to take that advice, and it is exhilarating!

In middle school English class, we had to memorize and recite the poem "The Road Not Taken" by Robert Frost. At the time, this seemed like a silly exercise, since I had no idea why that poem was so important. I know my teacher tried to help us figure out why it mattered, but without the life experience to apply to it, the poem meant little to me. It is ironic to me now, that after all these years, I find this poem so profound. If I could recall who my English teacher was, I would thank her for making me do this assignment. I especially like the ending, because it rings so true for my life thus far. I did not follow a traditional path—a path like my mother or my siblings, or even most of my friends. And yet, it has been an incredible path, filled with learning, growing, and hindsight into the reasons things happened the way they did. Every experience taught me something. And, in the words of Robert Frost, that has made all the difference.

THE ROAD NOT TAKEN
BY ROBERT FROST

Two roads diverged in a yellow wood,
And sorry I could not travel both
And be one traveler, long I stood
And looked down one as far as I could
To where it bent in the undergrowth;

Then took the other, as just as fair,
And having perhaps the better claim,
Because it was grassy and wanted wear;
Though as for that the passing there
Had worn them really about the same,

And both that morning equally lay
In leaves no step had trodden black.
Oh, I kept the first for another day!
Yet knowing how way leads on to way,
I doubted if I should ever come back.

I shall be telling this with a sigh
Somewhere ages and ages hence:
Two roads diverged in a wood, and I—
I took the one less traveled by,
And that has made all the difference.

—〰—

Looking for more ideas to orchestrate

your own Rebalancing Act?

Join our community at

www.carolenneking.com

to access resources and more!

—〰—

ACKNOWLEDGMENTS

This book was an idea fifteen years ago. I put it on the shelf until last year. I would like to thank all those who helped me turn this pipe dream into a reality.

Eric: Thank you for believing with me and encouraging me to move toward this dream. You made it safe for me to leave the known safety of a corporate job and venture into this new place far outside my comfort zone. I am thankful for the divine intervention that brought us together and for every single day I get the pleasure of being your wife. You are the other half of me, my person, my better half, and the love of my life and none of this would have been possible without you.

Bethany Bradsher: What can I even say about you? Thank you for being my best childhood friend who has remained a treasured friend for five decades. I have always been thankful that despite the miles through the years, we have always been able to pick up where we left off. You are one of the smartest, most caring, most exceptional all-around people I have ever had the pleasure of knowing, and I am delighted you came on this writing journey with me. I do not know how I would have ever pulled this together without your wisdom and guidance. You helped me tell the story, turned this into a first book that I am immensely proud of, and made the journey to publishing a lot of fun.

Bradley: You are intuitive and so very insightful. You are also the most loving, honorable, and caring son I could ever hope for. I know the Lord has amazing things planned for you and I am honored to watch you shine! The world needs more people like you in it. I love you to infinity! (I would say "and beyond," but as you reminded me when you were just a small child, there is nothing beyond infinity so Buzz made a mistake saying so.)

Bethany S: who knew when I began writing that my own daughter would be helping me with media. I would be honored to call you my "mini-me," but you have it far more together than I ever did at your age! I love seeing you thrive and look forward to seeing the places you will go. You have everything within you to be and do anything you aspire to. Thank you for all your proofreading, media calls, and time supporting me with this book. I love you to infinity!

Alyssa: You are such a wonderful addition to my family. I am very thankful you are my bonus daughter, and love you like my own flesh and blood! I have learned so much from you. Thank you for always being an encourager, for your creativity, and for showing us all what it looks like to follow your dreams wherever they may take you—and succeeding! Most of all, thank you for sharing your dad and your life with me. I love you so much!

Suzie, Melanie, and Greg: I am thankful for each of you and your uniqueness. I feel fortunate to have three siblings who I consider my dear friends. Each of us is different, but we also have a lot in common. I appreciate how each of you has provided advice, support, and a safe sounding board for me through the ups and downs in my life over the years. I would not be the person I am today without each of you, and I love you very much!

Alisa: I am not sure what I would have done without you in my life, both as a friend and as a colleague over the past few decades. You picked up the pieces during my divorce and ensured work still got done. You provided feedback and advice I needed to hear in a way that made me open to hearing it. You are my right hand and then some, and are one of the most giving, loving, and smartest people I've had the pleasure to know. I am so thankful for you!

Huntwick/Champions friends: meeting you when I was a new mom was an incredible blessing. How fortunate I am to have a tribe like you. I will always remember our preschool-era play dates at the park, where our kids played and we talked about everything under the sun for hours. I'm so glad I made time for our monthly bunco nights, even if we never played! I wonder if we ever could have imagined the journey we would take together, watching our kids grow up together, and now having the time to reward ourselves with girls' trips together! Thank you for always being there, being my constant sources for advice, support, and laughs. I love you all!

Interviewees: When I began seeking stories for this book, I had no idea where these would lead me. I find it surprising and exciting that half of you are people I don't even know, who took the time to provide me your insights based on a mutual friend's recommendation to do so. My hope is that your stories in this book honor your experiences and pay it forward to other women who can learn from your journey. Thank you for being the storytellers who brought this book to life!

Stephanie Dicken: You have such a gift for graphics! I am inspired and awed by your uncanny ability to visually represent my ideas in the most beautiful and professional manner. Thank you for bringing the concept of *The Rebalancing Act* to life in the design.

Tricia Brouk: It was through one of my interviews for this book that I was introduced to you. What a divinely orchestrated event! I am so thankful to have met you, learned from you, and to be partnering with you in this process. Thank you for seeing in me what I could barely see in myself, for taking my ideas and turning them into a plan, and for partnering with me to bring this book and my message to the world. The best is yet to come!

WORKS CITED

Thelatchedmama Instagram account, https://www.instagram.com/p/CgU6h1ouOb0/.

Taaffe, Ellen, "Do you Overprepare? Here are 4 Ways to Curb this Perfectionist Tendency," Kellogg Insight, June 1, 2023, https://insight.kellogg.northwestern.edu/article/overprepared-perfectionist-tendency-mirrored-door.

Morelock, Anna, "How Perfectionism Can Hurt a Team," InsightGlobal, June 7, 2023, https://insightglobal.com/blog/perfectionism-in-the-workplace/.

"7 Examples of Perfectionism in the Workplace," DecisionWise, https://decision-wise.com/resources/articles/7-behaviors-of-extreme-perfectionists-in-the-workplace/.

Benson, Etienne, "The many faces of perfectionism," Monitor on Psychology, November 2003, https://www.apa.org/monitor/nov03/manyfaces.

Piterman, Hannah, "The Leadership Challenge: Women in Management," Australian Government Department of Social Services, March 2008, https://www.dss.gov.au/our-responsibilities/women/publications-articles/economic-independence/the-leadership-challenge-women-in-management?HTML.

Rutherford, Christy, "The Vision Finder: 3 Reasons Women in Leadership Should Not Be More Vulnerable," January 10, 2020, https://www.linkedin.com/pulse/3-reasons-women-leadership-shouldnt-more-vulnerable/.

Lencioni, Patrick, "Five Dysfunctions of a Team," UMass Global CII, October 20, 2016, https://www.youtube.com/watch?v=wHpB1EBufFo.

Picchi, Aimee, "'Quiet quitting:' A revolution in how we work or the end of working hard?" cbsnews.com, August 24, 2022, https://www.cbsnews.com/news/what-is-quiet-quitting/.

Morin, Amy. "13 Things Mentally Strong People Don't Do," Inc.com, April 4, 2017, https://www.inc.com/amy-morin/13-things-mentally-strong-people-dont-do.html.

Printed in the USA
CPSIA information can be obtained
at www.ICGtesting.com
JSHW010720290824
68937JS00002B/5

9 781960 553041